Baby Names 2012

Eleanor Turner

white
LADDER

Acknowledgements

I would like to extend my utmost gratitude to Cerys Owen, Shelley Heck and Michael Turner for their contributions; without them this book would have been much shorter. My thanks are also given to Beth Bishop at Crimson Publishing for her patience and guidance throughout the project. Finally, the greatest thanks go to Owen Henri Turner, who grew patiently inside me while I wrote this book and waited to be born until I had chosen his name.

ISBN-13: 978 1 905410 90 3

Typeset by IDSUK (DataConnection) Ltd

Printed and bound in the United States of America by Sheridan Books Inc, Michigan

Contents

A note on how to use this book

While the author and publisher acknowledge that baby names vary widely in spelling and pronunciation, this book lists each name only once: under the most common initial and spelling. If a name has an alternative spelling with a different initial, it may be listed under that letter also.

Introduction

Did you know that the name Gavin was popular in South Dakota, but not in any other state?

Which celeb recently named their child Moroccan Scott?

And will the 'Twilight' effect on names continue into 2012, with names such as Bella, Taylor and even Cullen jumping up the charts?

Picking a name for your baby is one of the most enjoyable activities for a new parent, but it's also one of the most daunting. Sometimes choosing the right name is simply a case of hearing one you like and knowing instantly that you've chosen correctly. But, for the vast majority of parents the naming game gets far more complicated, when you start trying to please parents, grandparents, friends and siblings, while trying to avoid names that could be shortened into ridiculous nicknames or would make for funny initials.

You'll also probably want to choose something unique, but not *too* unique, or common but not *too* common. A name could be inspired by an admired celebrity, a sports star, or an influential historical or political figure. It could also come from the family tree, or follow a current babynaming trend. You also need to make sure you love it – you'll have to live with it forever! The possibilities are endless and it's understandable that it can set some parents into panic mode.

Well, never fear. *Baby Names 2012* is here to take you through your options and solve your baby-naming dilemmas. We update it every year, so it always includes the year's most popular names, celebrity choices, and names making a comeback. We've included dozens of lists to provide you with inspiration, and of course, some downright weird names children have been given over the years (usually by celebs).

Be sure to keep an eye out for all the facts and figures we've got for you – including what names are most popular in each state, so you can either go with the flow … or deliberately against it.

Remember, picking a baby name should be fun – so dip in, find some names you like and use the suggestions we've given you to work out if one of them is a winner!

part one

1

What was hot in 2011?

The rise of quirky names

Have you ever raised your eyebrows when you heard a friend's baby name choice? Statistics say you probably have.

Research shows that we are seeing more variation in the names parents are choosing than ever before. In the 1950s, the Top 25 boys' names and the Top 50 girls' names were given to 50% of all babies born in that decade. To reach the same figure now, you would have to include the Top 134 boys' names and the Top 320 girls'. This means that there is a far greater variety of names, spellings, pronunciations, and contracted names than ever before.

One explanation for this is that parents have begun to give their child a name *more* unusual than their own. A parent who has enjoyed their slightly unusual name will feel more confident about giving their offspring an even more unique name. If this trend continues into 2012 and beyond, you can be sure that names will get stranger and stranger ...

Some of the US's quirky baby names during the last year have included Chance, King, Rocco, and Titus for boys, and London, Miracle, Paisley, and Yaretzi for girls.

Traditional names continue to impress

What's interesting about recent trends, however, is that no matter how many new and unusual names enter the most popular baby name lists each year, you will always see a large number of babies given the same familiar and traditional names of the past. The Top 10 names for both boys and girls seem to stay pretty fixed each year, and 2011 was no different.

The names Jacob, Ethan, and Michael have appeared in the Top 10 boys' names each year since 2002, and the girls' names Isabella, Emma, and Emily have also stayed put. The name James, which has been the name most often given to baby boys over the last 100 years – an astonishing 4,868,315 little boys, in fact – has also remained in the Top 20 in 2011.

Top 10 baby boy names

1. Jacob
2. Ethan
3. Michael
4. Jayden
5. William

6. Alexander
7. Noah
8. Daniel
9. Aiden
10. Anthony

Top 10 baby girl names

1. Isabella
2. Sophia
3. Emma
4. Olivia
5. Ava

6. Emily
7. Abigail
8. Madison
9. Chloe
10. Mia

Aiden was the only new name among the Top 10 for either gender.

We've also seen traditional names re-enter the charts. Names such as Abraham, Ava and Josie had dropped out of mainstream use by the 1960s and become vastly unpopular, but in the last five years names ending in -a, -ie, and -en have started to see a resurgence, particularly as a spelling option for parents who like the sound of a traditional name but want to give it a modern twist. Other old-fashioned names, such as Daniel, Hannah, Sophia, and William, have climbed the popularity ranks in the Top 100 lists, joining such stalwarts as Joshua, Madison, Matthew, and Olivia.

The traditional name for baby boys in some Christian families has often been Noah, which has now become so popular a choice in the US that it entered the Top 10 for the first time last year.

Jacob and Isabella top the lists for the second year in a row. Incredibly, either Jacob or Michael has remained the top choice for parents of newborn baby boys in the United States for the last 50 years.

2011 popular newcomers

Boys	Girls
Bentley	Isla
Kellan	Adalyn
Kingston	Giuliana
Aiden	Olive
Ryker	Kinsley

The effects of pop culture

If the last few years have taught us anything about the power of pop culture on baby names, it's that parents are becoming more and more influenced by what they see and hear around them. 2011 was no different, with celebrities such as Justin Bieber, Miley Cyrus, Charlie Sheen, Natalie Portman dominating the headlines and affecting naming decisions the world over.

Growing in popularity

Boys	Girls
1. Bentley	1. Isla
2. Kellan	2. Tiana
3. Ryker	3. Giuliana
4. Aarav	4. Olive
5. Jax	5. Paisley
6. Beckett	6. Evangeline
7. Colt	7. Kinsley
8. Paxton	8. Kinley
9. Kingston	9. Maci
10. Lincoln	10. Adalyn

The name Bentley was the fastest-growing in popularity for little boys in 2011, and Maci for girls. This can be attributed in part to young mom Maci Bookout and the name she chose for her son on MTV shows *16 and Pregnant* and *Teen Mom*. Bentley rose to 101 in 2010, from 515 a year earlier, and Maci climbed to 232 from 655.

Entertainment reporter Giuliana Rancic should be thrilled to hear she's started a trend for naming little girls after her, as the name Giuliana is on the rise, as is the boys' name Kellan. This should come as no surprise, as Kellan Lutz, the actor who plays Emmett in the hugely popular Twilight series has shot to fame recently. Anything to do with Twilight seems to be touched by gold right now – the names Edward, Isabella and Jacob have all leapt in popularity. Even stranger, the last names of these characters have too: the name Cullen jumped 300 places in a single year.

Baby Names 2012

The name Isabella jumped from position 895 in 1990 to number 1 in 2011 thanks to the 'Twilight' effect.

As always, the names of movie stars and the characters they play entered our psyches in 2011. The whirlwind of awards season early in the year highlighted the talent and fame of several major newcomers, including Hailee Steinfeld and Jesse Eisenberg, and the rejuvenation of established careers, such as Natalie Portman's and Colin Firth's. The names of Academy Award winners have always been popular, and 2011 was no different, with the name Natalie staying put in the Top 20 and Hailey appearing at position 25. Even the name Colin, which was down to position 119 in 2007, has seen a surge in popularity.

The name Elvis dropped out of the top 1,000 US baby names in 2010, the first year it had not made the list since 1954.

The release of the eighth and final Harry Potter movie closed a chapter on the impressive climb to fame for the names Harry, Hermione, Ronald and Ginny, and it seems likely that these names will no longer appear in the Top 1,000 from 2012 onwards.

The 2009 Disney movie *The Princess and the Frog* proved popular with prospective parents – so much so that Tiana, the name of the main character, rocketed up the charts, and was one of the biggest gainers this year.

Actors from the TV show *Gossip Girl* are starting to make their presence known on the charts. The name Leighton, after actress Leighton Meester, appeared in the Top 1,000 for the first time in 2009 at position 669 and continues to rise; and the name Chase, after actor Chace Crawford, has been steadily climbing since the early 1990s and peaked at position 69 recently.

From *Modern Family*, actress Sofia Vergara's Latin spelling of the popular name Sophie has had an effect, coming in at position 36 last year – a jump of 60 places since 2003. The character of Quinn in *Glee* is responsible for more baby boys *and* girls having the same name in 2011.

However, a popular show does not always prove to be popular with baby name choices. The name Simon has not moved from below position 250 in the charts in the last 50 years, which might disappoint Simon Cowell (although he probably won't care!), and even Johnny Depp and Matt Damon's summer blockbusters didn't create a surge in the popularity of their names – although the names John and Matthew did both stay in the Top 20.

Colin Firth doesn't like his name, apparently. In 2011 he was quoted as saying: 'Colin is the sort of name you'd give your goldfish for a joke. I once saw an episode of *Blackadder* with a dachshund in it called Colin. It seemed his name alone was supposed to reduce you to fits of laughter.'

Celebrity power

As always, the world of celebrity continued to dominate choices made by parents, for better or worse.

The name Benjamin has grown in popularity after the birth of Gisele Bundchen and Tom Brady's baby boy in 2009, moving from position 27 to 20, and has also been given to John Travolta and Kelly Preston's little boy and NASCAR driver Jeff Gordon's son Leo Benjamin, both of whom were born in 2010. In the last year alone, a variation on the name Ava has been given to at least three new celebrity babies: Aviana Olea (Amy Adams' daughter), Grace Avery (Kevin Costner's baby girl) and Ava Grace (Melissa Rycroft's new arrival). Reese Witherspoon has been given credit for this surge: after naming her daughter Ava in 1999 after actress Ava Gardner, the name jumped from rank number 259 to number 9 in 2005 and has stayed in the top five ever since.

After Britney Spears named her second son Jayden James in 2006, the name became the second most popular name for baby boys in New York City.

Celebrity babies of the last year

Theodore (Ali Larter and Hayes MacArthur, Dec 2010)
Locklyn (Vince Vaughn and Kyla Weber, Dec 2010)
Ever Imre (Alanis Morissette and Mario Treadway, Dec 2010)
Zachary Jackson Levon (Elton John and David Furnish, Dec 2010)
Sadie Grace (Christina Applegate and Martyn Lenoble, Jan 2011)

Leo (Penelope Cruz and Javier Bardem, Jan 2011)
Flynn (Orlando Bloom and Miranda Kerr, Jan 2011)
Marlowe Rivers (Jason Schwartzman and Brady
 Cunningham, Jan 2011)
Max Ellington (Cynthia Nixon and Christine Marinoni,
 Feb 2011)
Ava Grace (Melissa Rycroft and Tye Strickland, Feb 2011)
Aiden (Rod Stewart and Penny Lancaster, Feb 2011)
Jackson Wright (John Henson and Jill Benjamin, Mar 2011)
Philip (Eva Herzigova and Gregorio Marsiaj, Mar 2011)
Skyler Morrison (Rachel Zoe and Rodger Berman,
 Mar 2011)
Monroe and Moroccan Scott (Mariah Carey and Nick
 Cannon, Apr 2011)
Bennett (Jane Krakowski and Robert Godley, Apr 2011)
Tate (Emma Bunton and Jade Jones, May 2011)
Cleo (David Schwimmer and Zoe Buckman, May 2011)
Bear Blu (Alicia Silverstone and Christopher
 Jarecki, May 2011)
Kroy Jagger (Kim Zolciak and Kroy Biermann, May 2011)
Willow Sage (Pink and Carey Hart, Jun 2011)
Agnes Lark (Jennifer Connelley and Paul Bettany,
 Jun 2011)

It's reassuring to know that even celebrities have a hard time deciding on baby names – in May 2010 Amanda Peet appeared on David Letterman's show to tell the world the name of her new daughter, and explained that she and her husband, David Benioff, had had a very difficult time settling on a final decision. Eventually, she said, they wrote the two names they were considering on two pieces of paper, and chose one at random. When it turned out to be Mya the actress got upset and felt they'd made the wrong choice, so they went with the other one instead: Molly June.

Although celebrities are often known for choosing highly original (or simply weird) names for their children, new arrivals in the last year or so have actually been given fairly normal names, and we are starting to see more traditional names gaining popularity with celebs. Variations on the names Olivia, James, Grace, and Maria are all hot picks at the moment, especially as middle names.

Take a look at the babies of several stars born in recent months: Eva Herzigova, Orlando Bloom and Christina Applegate. Each celeb chose a name which would not sound out of place in the playground of any school: Philip, Flynn and Sadie (which has jumped up 500 places in the rankings since 1982), respectively.

In fact, even the more unusual names on the roll-call for 2010/2011 aren't that strange: Locklyn, Aiden and Max for example. Of babies born recently, Alicia Keys and Alanis Morissette went with unique names that might raise a few eyebrows: Egypt Dauod Dean and Ever Imre – both little boys, and neither name making the Top 1,000 names over the last 100 years!

Mariah Carey and Nick Cannon's twins followed the trend of the wacky celeb baby names – baby girl Monroe named after Marilyn Monroe, and Moroccan Scott is named after the Moroccan Room in his parent's penthouse, where Nick proposed … and Scott is Nick's middle name. Mariah sent fans into a frenzy when she strung her name announcement out for hours, getting her followers on Twitter to guess, with a clue that they both begin with the letter M.

Crazy celebrity baby names of recent years

Apple (Gwyneth Paltrow and Chris Martin)

Blue Angel (U2's The Edge and Aislinn O'Sullivan)

Bluebell Madonna (Geri Halliwell)

Bodhi Hawn (Oliver Hudson and Erinn Bartlett)

Bronx Mowgli (Ashlee Simpson and Pete Wentz)

Brooklyn (David and Victoria Beckham – also parents to Romeo and Cruz)

Egypt Dauod Dean (Alicia Keys and Swizz Beatz)

Ever Imre (Alanis Morissette and Mario Treadway)

Ikhyd (M.I.A and Benjamin Brewer)

Kal-El (Nicholas Cage – Kal-El is Superman's original birth name)

Buddy Bear Maurice (Jules and Jamie Oliver – also parents to Daisy Boo, Poppy Honey, and Petal Blossom Rainbow)

Shiloh Nouvel (Brad Pitt and Angelina Jolie)

Sparrow (Nicole Richie and Joel Madden – also parents to Harlow)

Sunday Rose (Nicole Kidman and Keith Urban)

Suri (Tom Cruise and Katie Holmes)

Zuma Nesta Rock (Gwen Stefani and Gavin Rossdale)

Tom Cruise and Katie Holmes learnt a lesson about the woes of celebrity naming, when they found out their daughter Suri's name meant 'from Syria' and not 'princess' in Hebrew, as they'd thought.

State differences

What's interesting about US baby name statistics is that there is such variety in the popularity of names across different states and territories …

- The name Allison appears as the most popular name only in the District of Columbia, and yet the name Isabella appeared in almost every single Top 5 list in the country.

- While the names Ethan and Jacob were popular across the board, only parents in South Dakota chose to name their baby boys Gavin.

- Baby boys overwhelmingly received names such as Ethan, Liam or Logan, except in British Columbia, where Benjamin made the Top 5.

The most popular name in Texas is currently José, as 2,257 new babies born near the Mexico border can testify.

It makes sense that Spanish names are more popular the higher the Hispanic population, and this is likely to be in those border states in the South: the name Angel, for example, appears in both Texas and Arizona's Top 5 names for boys. It seems as though geography can have a major impact on baby-naming decisions, and population density can certainly change the rankings.

Find your state from the lists below – and make sure your baby won't have another 10 Isabellas or Jacobs in their class!

Top 5 Baby Boy Names by US State

State	Rank 1	Rank 2	Rank 3	Rank 4	Rank 5
Alabama	William	James	Jacob	Jackson	John
Alaska	Michael	Ethan	Logan	Samuel	Elijah
Arizona	Jacob	Alexander	Daniel	Angel	Anthony
Arkansas	William	Jacob	Ethan	Joshua	Jayden
California	Daniel	Anthony	Angel	Jacob	Alexander
Colorado	Alexander	Jacob	Noah	William	Benjamin
(Dist. of) Columbia	William	Michael	James	Alexander	Daniel
Connecticut	Michael	Ryan	Alexander	Matthew	Jayden
Delaware	Alexander	Michael	James	Jayden	Ethan
Florida	Jayden	Michael	Joshua	Jacob	Anthony
Georgia	William	Christopher	Joshua	James	Jayden
Hawaii	Ethan	Noah	Jayden	Joshua	Elijah
Idaho	Logan	Jacob	Ethan	William	Wyatt
Illinois	Alexander	Daniel	Jacob	Michael	Anthony
Indiana	Ethan	Noah	Jacob	Logan	Elijah
Iowa	Jacob	Ethan	Carter	Noah	William
Kansas	Ethan	William	Jacob	Alexander	Noah
Kentucky	Jacob	William	James	Ethan	Noah
Louisiana	Jayden	Ethan	Landon	Joshua	Noah
Maine	Noah	Logan	Jacob	Owen	Aiden
Maryland	Michael	Jayden	Joshua	Ethan	William
Massachusetts	Ryan	Jacob	William	Michael	Matthew
Michigan	Jacob	Ethan	Logan	Noah	Aiden
Minnesota	Logan	Benjamin	William	Ethan	Jacob
Mississippi	William	Jayden	James	Christopher	Joshua
Missouri	Jacob	Ethan	William	Jackson	Logan

What was hot in 2011?

State	Rank 1	Rank 2	Rank 3	Rank 4	Rank 5
Montana	Ethan	Wyatt	Logan	Landon	James
Nebraska	Alexander	Carter	Noah	William	Jacob
Nevada	Anthony	Jacob	Daniel	Michael	Alexander
New Hampshire	Logan	Jacob	Liam	Aiden	Ryan
New Jersey	Michael	Matthew	Anthony	Jayden	Ryan
New Mexico	Aiden	Noah	Joshua	Jacob	Gabriel
New York	Michael	Jayden	Matthew	Ethan	Daniel
North Carolina	William	Jacob	Christopher	Noah	Joshua
North Dakota	Ethan	Logan	Jack	Carter	Jacob
Ohio	Jacob	Noah	Ethan	Logan	William
Oklahoma	Ethan	Jacob	Noah	William	Joshua
Oregon	Alexander	Logan	Jacob	Daniel	Ethan
Pennsylvania	Michael	Jacob	Ethan	Logan	Matthew
Puerto Rico	Luis	Angel	Adrian	José	Diego
Rhode Island	Anthony	Jayden	Logan	Jacob	Michael
South Carolina	William	Jayden	Christopher	James	Jacob
South Dakota	Ethan	Noah	Gavin	Logan	Jackson
Tennessee	William	Jacob	Joshua	Noah	Ethan
Texas	José	Daniel	Jacob	Angel	Christopher
Utah	Ethan	William	Jacob	Isaac	James
Vermont	Noah	William	Owen	Logan	Aiden
Virginia	William	Jacob	Michael	Noah	Ethan
Washington	Alexander	Jacob	Ethan	William	Daniel
West Virginia	Jacob	Hunter	Ethan	Noah	Aiden
Wisconsin	Ethan	Jacob	Noah	Logan	Mason
Wyoming	Wyatt	William	Aiden	Jacob	Mason
Other US territories	Daniel	David	Joseph	Jayden	Aiden

Top 5 Baby Girl Names by US State

State	Rank 1	Rank 2	Rank 3	Rank 4	Rank 5
Alabama	Emma	Madison	Isabella	Ava	Anna
Alaska	Isabella	Sophia	Olivia	Abigail	Ava
Arizona	Isabella	Sophia	Emma	Mia	Emily
Arkansas	Emma	Madison	Addison	Isabella	Ava
California	Isabella	Sophia	Emily	Mia	Samantha
Colorado	Isabella	Olivia	Sophia	Abigail	Emma
(Dist. of) Columbia	Allison	Sophia	Ashley	Katherine	Abigail
Connecticut	Isabella	Olivia	Sophia	Ava	Emma
Delaware	Isabella	Olivia	Sophia	Abigail	Ava
Florida	Isabella	Sophia	Emma	Emily	Olivia
Georgia	Madison	Isabella	Emma	Olivia	Ava
Hawaii	Isabella	Sophia	Mia	Ava	Chloe
Idaho	Olivia	Emma	Isabella	Sophia	Addison
Illinois	Isabella	Olivia	Sophia	Emma	Emily
Indiana	Emma	Olivia	Isabella	Ava	Addison
Iowa	Ava	Olivia	Emma	Isabella	Addison
Kansas	Emma	Isabella	Ava	Olivia	Abigail
Kentucky	Emma	Isabella	Madison	Olivia	Abigail
Louisiana	Ava	Emma	Isabella	Madison	Olivia
Maine	Emma	Olivia	Isabella	Abigail	Madison
Maryland	Madison	Olivia	Ava	Isabella	Emma
Massachusetts	Olivia	Isabella	Sophia	Ava	Emma
Michigan	Olivia	Isabella	Ava	Emma	Madison
Minnesota	Olivia	Ava	Emma	Sophia	Isabella
Mississippi	Madison	Emma	Addison	Ava	Anna
Missouri	Emma	Olivia	Isabella	Ava	Madison

What was hot in 2011?

State	Rank 1	Rank 2	Rank 3	Rank 4	Rank 5
Montana	Emma	Isabella	Olivia	Ava	Madison
Nebraska	Addison	Isabella	Ava	Olivia	Emma
Nevada	Isabella	Sophia	Emma	Olivia	Emily
New Hampshire	Olivia	Isabella	Ava	Emma	Abigail
New Jersey	Isabella	Olivia	Sophia	Ava	Emily
New Mexico	Isabella	Olivia	Mia	Nevaeh	Sophia
New York	Isabella	Sophia	Olivia	Emma	Emily
North Carolina	Emma	Madison	Isabella	Ava	Abigail
North Dakota	Olivia	Ava	Emma	Ella	Isabella
Ohio	Isabella	Emma	Olivia	Ava	Madison
Oklahoma	Isabella	Emma	Addison	Madison	Abigail
Oregon	Emma	Isabella	Olivia	Emily	Sophia
Pennsylvania	Isabella	Olivia	Ava	Emma	Sophia
Puerto Rico	Alondra	Mia	Valeria	Kamila	Camila
Rhode Island	Isabella	Olivia	Sophia	Ava	Emma
South Carolina	Emma	Madison	Isabella	Olivia	Abigail
South Dakota	Emma	Ava	Isabella	Sophia	Alexis
Tennessee	Emma	Madison	Isabella	Olivia	Abigail
Texas	Isabella	Emily	Mia	Emma	Sophia
Utah	Olivia	Emma	Abigail	Brooklyn	Lily
Vermont	Emma	Ava	Isabella	Madison	Sophia
Virginia	Isabella	Madison	Emma	Olivia	Abigail
Washington	Isabella	Olivia	Sophia	Emma	Abigail
West Virginia	Madison	Isabella	Emma	Alexis	Emily
Wisconsin	Olivia	Isabella	Emma	Ava	Sophia
Wyoming	Isabella	Madison	Ava	Emma	Alexis
Other US territories	Ashley	Arianna	Gabriella	Alexis	Chloe

2

What does 2012 hold for baby names?

Will these trends continue?

Looking forward to 2012, we predict the trend for choosing either old fashioned or very unique names will continue. The Top 10 names will probably go largely unchanged for both boys and girls, but we may become even more varied in the names we give our children, and not just stick to the same safe names. There may also be a backlash against very popular names, as parents opt to not give their child the same name as four or five of their potential school friends.

As parents grow more globally aware and the demographics of North America change, we may see more culturally and ethnically diverse names appearing in these lists, such as

Fernanda and Mekhi. This has already started to happen with the name Maliyah, which jumped up a massive 342 positions in the last year, from 638 to 296.

Parents may also start looking further back into their family trees for inspiration, giving rise to many more African (Iman, Kwame), Asian (Mali, Thao), Scandinavian (Karita, Larson), and Middle English names (Avery, Tate). Our heritage is such a hugely important part of life in the US that it would be very appropriate for parents to choose the name of an ancestor for their new baby.

It seems likely that parents will continue the recent trend of naming their children shortened versions of longer, more traditional names. The name Maisie, for example, is a shortened version of Margaret, while Bobby is more usually written as Robert. The cult of celebrity and TV characters may be responsible for this, as viewers become more familiar with nicknames than actual names – Charlie (Sheen) for example, or Bella (Isabella Swan, from 'Twilight').

Predicted 2012 Top 10 baby names

Boys	Girls
1. Jacob	1. Sophia
2. Ethan	2. Isabella
3. Alexander	3. Emma
4. Michael	4. Olivia
5. William	5. Ava
6. Daniel	6. Madison
7. Jayden	7. Emily
8. Joshua	8. Abigail
9. Noah	9. Chloe
10. Anthony	10. Mia

2012 events

Other influences on the names parents choose in 2012 will come from the worlds of sport and politics.

The Summer Olympics will be hosted in 2012 by the city of London, in the UK. It stands to reason that the heroes of these games will inspire some parents to name their children after them: Michael Phelps' record-breaking eight gold medals at the Beijing 2008 Olympics certainly had an influence, as did Shaun White's performance in the 2010 Winter Olympics in Vancouver – the name Shaun jumped up 200 places in popularity in 2010.

The eyes of soccer fans will be resting on the outcome of the UEFA EURO 2012, hosted this time in Poland and Ukraine. Successful soccer stars often have babies named after them, with names such as Wayne (Rooney), Thierry (Henry) and Landon (Donovan) all peaking in popularity during sporting events.

Every year baby names are influenced by the success of teams and players across the spectrum of sporting events, and there is no reason to suggest 2012 will be any different. The winners of the 108th World Series, Superbowl XLVI, the All-Star Stanley Cup game hosted this time in Ottawa, and even the World Chess Championship, may have an impact – you never know! Ben Roethlisberger, quarterback for the Pittsburgh Steelers, saw his name jump to position 20 in the US national statistics the same year his team won their sixth Superbowl title in 2009.

2012 will see an important political battle take place in November: the presidential election. Whether you plan on voting for a Democrat, Republican or Independent, the outcome of the election will be closely observed by the media. While you might think that a president's name automatically means a surge in popularity during their term, you'd be mistaken – the name George actually declined in popularity following President George W. Bush's win in 2000, and President Barack Obama's name has yet to enter even the Top 1,000.

Interestingly, there is a trend of naming babies after the *children* of politicians – Barack Obama's daughters are named Maliyah and Sasha, and a variation of both of these appear in the Top 100 names for girls.

Sometimes the phenomenon of naming babies after the children of politicians doesn't even have to mean the successful ones: Sarah Palin's attempt to become the vice-president in 2008 fixed the world's eyes upon her, and led to her five children becoming somewhat famous in their own right. Her daughter Bristol, who competed in the 11th season of *Dancing with the Stars* in 2010, saw her name enter the Top 1,000 for the first time in 2009, and Piper, Palin's fourth child, has seen her name steadily increase in popularity since the family came to the nation's attention in 2007.

Significant dates in 2012

Significant anniversaries can potentially influence baby names. In 2012 this includes the 200th anniversary of the

What does 2012 hold for baby names?

War of 1812, the 100th anniversary of the sinking of the
Titanic, 100 years since the introduction of Lifesavers candy
to the world, and 100 years since the first list of birthstones
was released by the Jewelers of America association. It will
also be the English author Charles Dickens' 200th birthday
and 150 years since the birth of composer Claude Debussy,
as well as 100 years since New Mexico and Arizona joined
the Union to become states.

Celebrating their first wedding anniversary, but 11 years
since they first met, will be Prince William and Catherine.
After all the majesty and ceremony during their wedding in
2011, it will be interesting to see how they, and the media,
report back on their first year of marriage … and if we hear
of their own baby name choices!

Of course, the year 2012 cannot be discussed without
some mention of the significance of the Mayan Calendar,
which ends on December 21, 2012 and supposedly sym-
bolizes the end of days. However you interpret the theories
and mystery surrounding the Mayan Calendar, you can be
sure you'll hear a lot about it in the months preceding
December.

Don't be surprised, therefore, if the names Charles, Claude,
Rose and Jack (from the movie *Titanic*), William, Kate,
Maya, and even some names of birthstones all jump in
popularity in 2012. The very fact that these names will be
brought to the nation's attention by the media will mean
parents will start to consider them as potential candidates,
even if they would never have considered them previously.

2012 anniversary names

Boys	Girls
Charles	Arizona
Claude	Catherine
Garnet	Kate
Jack	Maya
William	Pearl
	Rose
	Ruby

The influence of pop culture will continue

As we've seen this year, pop culture will be perhaps the most prominent influence on baby names in the coming year. Celebrity couples expecting babies in late 2011 and 2012 include Jessica Alba and Cash Warren, Mel B and Stephen Belafonte, and Kate Hudson and Matt Bellamy. The name choices these celebrities make may well influence the choices made by the general population.

Reality series will continue to influence our decisions – the name Khloe (spelt with a K) jumped in popularity after the *Keeping Up with the Kardashians* star began her own reality show with husband Lamar Odom in 2011. The year 2012 will no doubt see another wave of reality TV shows and their assorted crews of tearaways and rich teens, so it will be interesting to see if the *Jersey Shore* kids or *Real Housewives* cast influence baby names in the year ahead.

What does 2012 hold for baby names?

Simon Cowell's *The X Factor* involved much hype in 2011, but will its judges, Paula Abdul and Nicole Scherzinger see their names rise in popularity in 2012?

One of *Glee's* most talked-about characters, Quinn, named her baby Beth. However, while the name Beth might not have risen in popularity recently, the name Quinn definitely has! It will be among the Top 50 names for baby girls in 2012, up from position 258 in 2009.

The movie version of J.R.R. Tolkien's classic book *The Hobbit* is on schedule to hit movie theatres in 2012, and if the influence of the *Lord of the Rings* flicks are anything to go by, *The Hobbit* will also be huge! You probably won't see many children named Bilbo Baggins come 2013, but there may be a few little girls named Saoirse or little boys named Elijah, after the actors Saoirse Ronan and Elijah Wood. Even Martin Freeman, who will be playing the part of Bilbo Baggins, might see his name appearing more frequently – although the last time Martin was in the Top 100 was 1970.

Other movies set to be released in 2012 include *Men in Black 3*, *Bourne Legacy*, *Breaking Dawn Part 2*, and *Life of Pi*. At the time of printing there is also speculation that a widely anticipated new TV series about the end of the world according to the Mayan calendar, called *2012*, will be hitting the small screen, and is set to become as addictive as *Lost*. Watch out for the names of characters from these shows, or the actors playing those characters, to suddenly become immensely popular!

Expected new arrivals in 2011/2012

Natalie Portman and Benjamin Millepied	(Spring 2011)
Victoria and David Beckham	(July 2011)
Selma Blair and Jason Bleick	(July 2011)
Kate Hudson and Matt Bellamy	(Summer 2011)
Ivanka Trump and Jared Kushner	(Summer 2011)
Jewel and Ty Murray	(Summer 2011)
Alyssa Milano and David Bugliari	(Summer 2011)
Mel B and Stephen Belafonte	(Summer 2011)
Selma Blair and Jason Bleick	(Summer 2011)
Jessica Alba and Cash Warren	(Fall 2011)
Mya Rudolph and Paul Thomas Anderson	(Fall 2011)
Kimberley Stewart and Benicio Del Toro	(Fall 2011)
Guy Ritchie and Jacqui Ainsley	(Fall 2011)
Johnny Knoxville and Naomi Nelson	(Fall 2011)
January Jones	(Fall 2011)
Tina Fey	(Fall 2011)
Kimberley Stewart and Benicio del Toro	(Fall 2011)
Tori Spelling and Dean McDermott	(Fall 2011)

3

How to choose a name

Top tips on choosing a name

- **Fall in love with the name(s) you've chosen.** If you plough through this book and none of them jump off the page at you, then you probably haven't found the right one yet. Likewise, if a relative, friend, or even your spouse suggests a name and you wrinkle your nose up every time you hear it, it's also not the name for your baby. Pick a name that makes you smile because if you love it, hopefully your child will too.

- **Don't listen to other people.** Sometimes, grandparents and friends will offer 'advice' to you during this time which may not always be welcome. This is worth bearing in mind if you've fallen in love with a name and it's either slightly unusual or doesn't follow the set pattern your partner's family have used for the last 50 years. Sharing your choice of name with other people can lead them to criticize it, which you'd probably rather not hear if you've got your heart set on it. Also, if you're bucking with tradition and don't plan on calling your newborn after their great-great-great-grandfather, keep it a secret until after the birth. Trust your own instincts and remember: no-one will really care once they see your baby. Its name will simply be its name.

- **Find a name with meaning.** Having a name that has a back story helps your child understand their significance in the world, so whether you name them after a religious saint or prophet, an important political figure or a hero in a Greek tragedy, ensure they know where their name came from. They may just be inspired to be as great as their namesake.

- **Have fun.** Picking out names should be a fun process. Laughing at the ones you'd never dream of choosing can really help you narrow it down to the ones you would. You can also experiment with different spellings, pronunciations or variations of names you like, or go to places where you might feel inspired.

- **Expand your mind.** Don't rule out the weird ones just yet! As a teenager I went to school with a girl named Siam. Her parents had conceived her on a honeymoon trip to Thailand and given her the country's old name as a result. She loved growing up and having an unusual name, as I'm sure Brooklyn Beckham (David and Victoria Beckham's son) and Bronx Wentz (Ashley Simpson and Pete Wentz's son) do too. Also, don't be afraid to play around with spellings and pronunciations, even if the results are a little less than conformist. The name Madison, for example, could be spelt Maddison, Madyson, Maddiesun or even Maddeesunn if you so choose, although you might want to be careful you don't saddle your child with an impossible name to spell, pronounce *and* fit onto a passport application form.

The shortest baby names are only two letters long (Al, Ed, Jo and Ty), but the longest could be any length imaginable. Popular 11 letter-long names include Bartholomew, Christopher, Constantine and Maximillian.

- **Try it out.** While you're pregnant, talk to your baby and address it using a variety of your favorite names to see if it responds. There are numerous stories of names being chosen because the baby kicked when it was called Charlie or Aisha, but was suspiciously silent when it was called Dexter or Mildred, so see if it has a preference! Try writing names down and sticking them to your fridge, or saying one out loud enough times to see if you ever get sick of it.

- **What if you can't agree?** This is probably the trickiest problem in the baby-naming process to solve. It's wise to research a number of names you and your partner are both interested in and make a point of discussing your reasons for liking or disliking them long before the baby is due to be born. The labor and delivery room is probably not the best time to argue as you'll both be tired, emotional, and at least one of you will be in pain. Avoid sticking to your guns on a name one of you really isn't happy with because it might lead to resentment down the line, with your baby caught in the middle. You could try compromising and picking two middle names so you both have a name in there you love, or you could each have five names you're allowed to 'veto' but no more. Whichever way you go about it, it is important that you both eventually agree on the name you are giving your baby, even if it means losing out on that one you've had your heart set on for a while.

Popular names from the past

Boys	Girls
Abraham	Agatha
Arthur	Bertha
Edmund	Clara
Emmett	Edith
Franklin	Gladys
Gilbert	Mabel
Jasper	Pearl
Neville	Theodora
Percival	Wilhelmina
Vincent	Winifred

Think to the future

One important aspect of naming your child is thinking ahead to their future. Will the name you've chosen stand the test of time? Will names popular in 2012 remain popular in 2040? Will they be able to confidently enter a room and give a crucial business presentation with an awkward or unpronounceable name? Will they be able to hand their business card over to a potential client without that client looking bemused every time? Would you want to try catching criminals as Sheriff Apple Blossom or have other politicians take you seriously with a name like Senator Lil' Kim Scarlett? Even on a smaller scale, can they survive the potential minefields of elementary school and junior high with a name that could be easily shortened to something embarrassing?

Banned names

The following names were all banned by registration officials in New Zealand:

Cinderella Beauty Blossom
Fat Boy
Fish and Chips (twins)
Keenan Got Lucy
O.crnia
Sex Fruit
Stallion
Talula Does The Hula From Hawaii
Twisty Poi
Yeah Detroit

This was because New Zealand law prevents parents from giving their children names which would cause offence or are more than 100 characters long.

Allowed names

These names, however, were all permitted by the same officials:

All Blacks

Benson and Hedges (twins)

Ford Mustang

Kaos

Masport and Mower (twins)

Midnight Chardonnay

Number 16 Bus Shelter

Spiral Cicada

Superman (changed from 4real)

Violence

French law prohibits all names other than those on an approved list.

Stereotypes – true or false?

Will the name you choose actually affect your child's life? Will names that seem clever make your child brainier? Will names with positive meanings make your child into a happier person? The answer is … possibly.

Some experts believe that parents who choose inspirational names for their offspring (Destiny, Serenity, Unique) or names of products they would like to own (Armani, Jaguar, Mercedes) are projecting a future onto their child for them to aspire to, and therefore help shape their child's life. There's no scientific evidence to prove that this actually works – but feel free to give it a go!

Inspirational names

Destiny	Joy
Happy	Peace
Heaven	Serenity
Hope	Unique
Innocence	Unity

Future aspirations names

Armani	Ferrari
Aston	Jaguar
Bugatti	Mercedes
Chanel	Porsche
Dolce	Prada

What is certain is that people have very real perceptions about names. Typically, judgments are made before a person is met, such as at job interviews or in school. A 2009 survey of 3,000 teachers found that 49% of teachers make assumptions about their pupils based on their name. One in three admitted that certain names spell a troublemaker to them, including Callum, Brandon, Chelsea and Aleisha, while the names Christopher, Edward, Rebecca and Charlotte were assumed to belong to brighter children.

Personality and character have a far greater influence than name alone and after a while, a name becomes just a name.

Ivy League names

Alcott	Graydon
Arthur	Katherine
Beatrice	Martha
Caroline	Robert
Charles	Victoria

Names which mean 'clever'

Abner	Shanahan
Cassidy	Todd
Haley	Ulysses
Penelope	Washington
Portia	Wylie

Quirky names

There are lots of advantages to having a quirky name. For one thing, your child's name will never be forgotten by other people, and if they do something influential with their life their name could become inspirational for other parents to name their children. On the other hand, a quirky name often requires a quirky personality. If you don't think your genes could stand up to a name like Satchel or Kerensa, perhaps it's time to think of one a little more run-of-the-mill.

A quirky name often says more about the parents than the child, whose own personalities may affect the personality of their child in a significant way. A conventional family who names their baby John will probably find he becomes a conventional child, whereas a quirky family who names their baby Zanzibar will also find he develops a quirky personality. The name itself is not the leading factor; it's the quirky or conventional behavior encouraged by the parents who chose the name that is.

Children who are told they have inherited an ancestor's name or are named after an influential character from history seem to be more driven and focused than children who are told disappointingly, 'We just liked the sound of it'. As a parent, therefore, it seems it's okay to pick an unusual name if you have a story or reason behind it. So naming your child Atticus (after Atticus Finch from Harper Lee's *To Kill A Mockingbird*, known for being a strong and moral character) may not be a bad idea …

What not to call your child ...

In Pennsylvania in December 2008 there was a case of a supermarket bakery refusing to ice the words 'Happy Birthday, Adolf Hitler' onto a three-year-old's birthday cake, despite never having met the child it was intended for. The parents were able to eventually fulfill the order at another shop, but as a result of the publicity surrounding the event Social Services were called in to assess the child's home and Adolf, along with his siblings JoyceLynn Aryan Nation and Honszlynn Hinler Jeannie, were taken into care.

Controversial names adopted by real people

Adolf Hitler
Beelzebub
Desdemona
Hannibal Lecter
Himmler
Jezebel
Lucifer
Mussolini
Stalin
Voldemort

While avoiding any kind of possible connection to a fictional character is nigh on impossible, you can help make things easier for your child by educating them about their namesake and encouraging them to read more about them. Stay up-to-date with new cartoons and children's characters in 2012 to prepare both yourself and your child for toddlerdom and childhood. That way they can be proud of their name and have ammunition if things get rough in the schoolyard.

Cartoon characters named after real people

Yogi Bear (named after baseball player Yogi Berra)

Alvin, Simon and Theodore Chipmunk (named after record executives)

Garfield (named after creator Jim Davis's grandfather)

Calvin and Hobbes (named after John Calvin [theologian] and Thomas Hobbes [philosopher])

Rock Lee (from *Naruto*, named after Bruce Lee)

Alexander Lemming (from *The Beano*, named after scientist Alexander Fleming)

Jimmy Neutron (named after the scientist James Chadwick, whose nickname was Jimmy Neutron)

Oscar (from *Cerebus*, named after writer Oscar Wilde)

Homer, Marge, Lisa and Maggie Simpson (named after creator Matt Groening's family members)

Teenage Mutant Ninja Turtles (all named after Renaissance painters: Raphael, Michelangelo, Donatello and Leonardo)

Nicknames

Nicknames are unavoidable. They can range from the common – Mike from Michael, Sam from Samantha – to the trendy, funny or downright insulting.

Don't be put off though if the name you love has an unfortunate nickname associated with it – if you don't encourage the use of nicknames, chances are one won't stick. Another way to avoid embarrassing nicknames is to select one for your child that you actually like so that others don't even get a mention. Call your daughter Elizabeth by the name Liz, Lizzie or Libby if you don't like Betty or Beth, and no-one will even consider the alternatives.

You can pre-empt possible nicknames to some extent by saying the name you've chosen out loud and trying to find rhymes for it. This is a clever way to avoid playground chants and nursery rhyme-type insults, such as Dora the Explorer or Georgie Porgie. But don't be too concerned about playground chants – most children are subjected to it at some point and emerge unscathed.

A Chinese couple were prevented from naming their child '@' in 2007, despite their reasoning that it was simply a modern choice of name in this technological age.

Your last name

Try to avoid first names that might lead to unfortunate phrases when combined with your last name, to prevent a lifetime of embarrassment for your child. The best way to work out if this might happen is to write down all the names you like alongside your child's last name and have someone else read them out loud. This second pair of eyes and ears might just spot something you didn't.

Unfortunate first name/last name combinations

Anna Sasin	Isabella Horn
Barb Dwyer	Justin Time
Barry Cade	Mary Christmas
Ben Dover	Oliver Sutton
Duane Pipe	Paige Turner
Grace Land	Russell Sprout
Harry Rump	Stan Still

There is also the danger of your child being subjected to having a spoonerism made out of their name, where the first letters or syllables get swapped around to form new words. An unfortunate and recent example of this would be Angelina Jolie and Brad Pitt's daughter Shiloh, whom they named Shiloh Jolie-Pitt to avoid the inevitable Shiloh Pitt spoonerism.

The micro-blogging site Twitter has recently become a hot spot for spoonerisms, with celebrites such as Justin Bieber and Nick Jonas calling each other 'Bustin Jieber' and 'Jick Nonas'. No-one ever said spoonerisms have to make sense …

Famous name spoonerisms

Justin Bieber (bustin jieber)
Shirley Bassey (burly chassis)
Gene Kelly (keen jelly)
Jude Law (lewd jaw)
Nick Jonas (jick nonas)
Paul Walker (wall porker)
Sarah Palin (para sailing)
Shiloh Pitt (pile o' s***)

Initials

What last name will your baby have? Will it lend itself easily to amusing acronyms when coupled with certain first and middle names? My brother-in-law was going to be called Andrew Steven Schmitt before he was born, until his parents realized at the last minute what his initials would spell ...

It's worth taking the time to think about how credit cards display names or seeing your child's name written out on a form. Nobody should have to go through life known as S. Lugg because their parents didn't think that far ahead.

Amusing initials

Earl E. Bird

Kay F. Cee

I. P. Freely

Al E. Gador

Angie O. Graham

S. Lugg

Warren T.

I.C. Blood

H. I. Vee

Gene E. Yuss

Amusing acronyms of real people

Filipe Bernardo Iñigo – FBI

Sally Therese Donaghue – STD

Tiffany Nancy Truman – TNT

Jake Clive Baxter – JCB

David Vernon Durante – DVD

Victoria Helen Smith – VHS

Jennifer Paige Garrett – JPG

George Barry Holmes – GBH

Across the US there are people whose initials spell out three letter words – from RAT and FAG to FAB or POP – and some are better than others so do check.

Using family names

Some families have a strong tradition of using names for babies that come from the family tree. There are instances where naming your son Augustine VIII is simply not an option; it's a rule. Another way families do this is to give children the name of their parent of the same sex and add 'Junior' (Jr) to the end. This could potentially create a problem if that child then decides to carry on the tradition and name their child after themselves – after all, who wants to be known as Frederick Jr Jr?

There are pros and cons with using family names:

- Pro: Your child will feel part of a strong tradition, which will create a sense of security for them and help make them feel a complete member of the family.

- Pro: If you're having a problem selecting a name you and your partner both agree on, this is a very simple solution and will make your new child's family very happy.

- Con: You might not actually like the name that's being passed down. Naming your child the 12th Thumbelina in a row might not actually hold the same attraction for you as for the generation before.

- Con: Another drawback could be if the cultural associations with that name have changed in your lifetime and it is no longer appropriate.

One way to include a family name is to compromise. You could use the name as a middle name, or refer to your baby by a nickname instead.

Top 10 US baby boy names

1900	1950	2000
John	James	Jacob
William	Robert	Michael
James	John	Matthew
George	Michael	Joshua
Charles	David	Christopher
Robert	William	Nicholas
Joseph	Richard	Andrew
Frank	Thomas	Joseph
Edward	Charles	Daniel
Henry	Gary	Tyler

Top 10 US baby girl names

1900	1950	2000
Mary	Linda	Emily
Helen	Mary	Hannah
Anna	Patricia	Madison
Margaret	Barbara	Ashley
Ruth	Susan	Sarah
Elizabeth	Nancy	Alexis
Florence	Deborah	Samantha
Ethel	Sandra	Jessica
Frances	Carol	Elizabeth
Lillian	Kathleen	Taylor

Spellings and pronunciation

Once you've finally agreed upon a name, it's time to consider how you wish it to be spelt and pronounced. Some
parents love experimenting with unusual variations of traditional names, while others prefer for names to be instantly
recognizable.

Try to avoid making a common name too long or too
unusual in its spelling as this will be the first thing your
child learns how to write. They will also have to spell it out
constantly during their lifetime, as other people misspell or
mispronounce their name. Substituting the odd 'i' for a 'y'
isn't too bad, but turning the name Jonathan into Jonnayth-
anne doesn't do anyone any favors.

The US has seen an increase in 'text speak' spellings

An	Helin
Camron	Jayk
Conna	Lora
Ema	Patryk
Esta	Samiul
Flicity	Summa

A palindrome name is a name that is spelt the same
backwards and forwards, as with Bob, Elle, Eve and
Hannah.

Middle names

The use of middle names is generally acknowledged to be standard practice in North America these days. In fact, it has become fairly uncommon to name a child *without* a middle name. A middle name can have just as much of an impact as a first name, so your choice for your own baby should be made as carefully as their first name.

Here are some common trends in 2012 to help you choose:

- **Opposite-length names**. It has become very popular to give a child either a long first name and short middle name (eg Jennifer Ruth, Nicholas John) and vice versa.

- **Name from the family tree**. Honoring your ancestors is another popular trend for 2012. Parents are frequently looking back to their own lineage for interesting, unusual or influential names. It is becoming more and more common to give a parents' first name as a middle name to newborns.

- **Unusual names**. Parents who like a quirky name but aren't quite brave enough to give it to their child as a first name are using it as a middle name.

The British teenager named **Captain Fantastic Faster Than Superman Spiderman Batman Wolverine Hulk And The Flash Combined**, changed his name from George Garratt in 2008. He claims to have the longest name in the world. If he does then he replaces

Texan woman **Rhoshandiatellyneshiaunneveshenk Koyaanisquatsiuth Williams,** whose 57-letter name pales in comparison to Captain's 81.

Many people actually choose to go by their middle name instead of their forename, so it could be seen as a safety net if you're worried your child won't like their name. In fact, you probably know someone in your family or workplace that has always been known as Ed or Sam when their name is actually James Edward Jones or Felicity Samantha Taylor.

Celebrities who go by middle names

Antonio Banderas (José Antonio Dominguez Banderas)
Bob Marley (Nesta Robert Marley)
Dakota Fanning (Hannah Dakota Fanning)
Will Ferrell (John William Ferrell)
Kelsey Grammar (Allen Kelsey Grammar)
Ashton Kutcher (Christopher Ashton Kutcher)
Hugh Laurie (James Hugh Calum Laurie)
Evangeline Lilly (Nicole Evangeline Lilly)
Brad Pitt (William Bradley Pitt)
Brooke Shields (Christa Brooke Camille Shields)
Reese Witherspoon (Laura Jean Reese Witherspoon)

Naming twins and more

If you have discovered you are expecting multiples, congratulations! Naming multiples needn't be any different to naming a single child … unless you want it to be. You could stick to the same process everyone else does, by picking an individual name for each individual child. In January 2009 Octomom Nadya Suleman, chose eight different names for her octuplets, although they do all sound reasonably similar: Isaiah, Jeremiah, Jonah, Josiah, Maliah, McCai, Nariah and Noah.

Twin names with the same meaning

Bernard and Brian (strong)

Daphne and Laura (laurel)

Deborah and Melissa (bee)

Dorcas and Tabitha (gazelle)

Elijah and Joel (God)

Eve and Zoe (life)

Irene and Salome (peace)

Lucius and Uri (light)

Lucy and Helen (light)

Sarah and Almira (princess)

Another option is to go with a theme. Try anagrams or names in reverse, or give each child the same initials or names with the same meaning. You could even do this if you're not expecting multiples, like the Duggar family of Arkansas, who have given each of their 19 children the initial 'J' – Joshua, Jana, John-David, Jill, Jessa, Jinger, Joseph, Josiah, Joy-Anna, Jedidiah, Jeremiah, Jason, James, Justin, Jackson, Johannah, Jennifer, Jordyn-Grace and Josie!

Mariah Carey and Nick Cannon chose to use names starting with the same letter when naming their twins. Before announcing the names, Nick posted a clue to the names on

Twitter, 'So we r bout 2 reveal the actual names and b4 we tell em 2 our friends etc. both begin w/M's!!!!' The couple then announced the arrival of Monroe and Moroccan Scott.

Popular twin names in 2012

Brandon and Brian

Daniel and David

Ella and Emma

Faith and Hope

Gabriella and Isabella

Isaac and Isaiah

Jacob and Joshua

Madison and Morgan

Matthew and Michael

Taylor and Tyler

Celebrity twin names of the past few years

Adalynn and Noah (Chris and Deanna Daughtry)

Darby and Sullivan (Patrick Dempsey and Jillian Fink)

Eddy and Nelson (Celine Dion and Rene Angelil)

Eden and Savannah (Marcia Cross and Tom Mahoney)

Hazel and Phinnaeus (Julia Roberts and Danny Moder)

Gideon and Harper (Neil Patrick Harris and David Burtka)

Jesse and Journey (Jenna Jameson and Tito Ortiz)

Max and Bob (Charlie Sheen and Brooke Mueller)

Max and Emme (Jennifer Lopez and Marc Anthony)
Vivienne Marcheline and Knox Leon (Angelina Jolie and Brad Pitt)
Monroe and Moroccan Scott (Mariah Carey and Nick Cannon)

Names for triplets

Abel, Bela and Elba (anagrams)
Aidan, Diana and Nadia (anagrams)
April, May and June (months)
Amber, Jade and Ruby (jewels)
Amy, May and Mya (anagrams)
Ava, Eva and Iva (similar)
Daisy, Lily and Rose (flowers)
Jay, Raven and Robin (birds)
Leah, Lianne and Liam (similar)
Olive, Violet and Sage (colors)

part two

Boys' Names

A Boys' names

Aaron

Hebrew, meaning 'mountain of strength'.

Abasi

Egyptian, meaning 'male'.

Abdiel

Biblical, meaning 'servant of God'.

Abdul

Arabic, meaning 'servant'. Often followed with a suffix indicating who Abdul is the servant of (eg Abdul-Basit, servant of the creator).

Abdullah

Arabic, meaning 'servant of God'.

Abe

Hebrew, from Abraham, meaning 'father'.

Abel

Hebrew, meaning 'breath' or 'breathing spirit'. Associated with the Biblical son of Adam and Eve who was killed by his brother Cain.

Abelard

German, meaning 'resolute'.

Aberforth

Gaelic, meaning 'mouth of the river Forth'. Name of Dumbledore's brother in the Harry Potter series.

A

Abner

Hebrew, meaning 'father of light'.

Abraham

Hebrew, meaning 'exalted father'.

Absalom
(alt. Absalon)

Hebrew, meaning 'father/ leader of peace'.

Acacio

Greek origin, meaning 'thorny tree'. Now widely used in Spain.

Ace

English, meaning 'number one' or 'the best'.

Achebe

Nigerian. Last name of famous writer Chinua Achebe.

Achilles

Greek, mythological hero of Trojan war, whose heel was his only weak spot.

Achim

Hebrew, meaning 'God will establish' or Polish, meaning 'The Lord exalts'.

Ackerley

Old English, meaning 'oak meadow'. Often used as last name, many similarly spelt variants.

Adalberto

Germanic/Spanish, meaning 'nobly bright'.

Adam

Hebrew, meaning 'man' or 'earth'. First man to walk the earth, accompanied by Eve.

Adão

Portuguese variant of Adam, meaning 'earth'.

Addison

Old English, meaning 'son of Adam'. Also used as a female name.

Ade

African, meaning 'peak' or 'pinnacle'.

Adelard

Teutonic, meaning 'brave' or 'noble'.

Adelbert

Old German form of Albert.

Aden

Gaelic, meaning 'fire'.

Adin

Hebrew, meaning 'slender' or 'voluptuous'. Also Swahili, meaning 'ornamental'.

Aditya

Sanskrit, meaning 'belonging to the sun'.

Adlai

Hebrew, meaning 'God is just', or sometimes 'ornamental'.

Adler

Old German, meaning 'eagle'.

Adley

English, meaning 'son of Adam'.

Admon

Hebrew origin, variant of Adam meaning 'earth'. Also the name of a red peony.

Adolph
(alt.Adolfo)

Old German, meaning 'noble majestic wolf'. Popularity of the name plummeted after the Second World War, for obvious reasons.

Adonis

Phoenician, meaning 'Lord'.

Movie inspirations

Anakin (Star Wars)
Edward (Twilight)
Forrest (*Forrest Gump*)
Harry (Harry Potter)
Indiana (*Raiders of the Lost Ark*)
Inigo (*Princess Bride*)
Korben (*The Fifth Element*)
Marty (*Back to the Future*)
Red (*The Shawshank Redemption*)
Vito (*The Godfather*)

A

Adrian

Latin origin, meaning 'from Hadria', a town in northern Italy.

Adriel

Hebrew, meaning 'of God's flock'.

Aeneas

Greek/Latin origin, meaning 'to praise'. Name of the hero who founded Rome in Virgil's *Aeneid*.

Aeson

Greek origin, father of Jason.

Afonso

Portuguese, meaning 'eager noble warrior'.

Agamemnon

Greek, meaning 'leader of the assembly'. Figure in mythology, commanded the Greeks at the siege of Troy.

Agathon

Greek, meaning 'good' or 'superior'.

Agustin

Latin/Spanish, meaning 'venerated'.

Ahab

Hebrew, meaning 'father's brother'. Pleasant way to address an uncle.

Ahijah

Hebrew, meaning 'brother of God' or 'friend of God'.

Ahmed

Arabic/Turkish, meaning 'worthy of praise'.

Aidan

Gaelic, meaning 'little fire'.

Aidric

Old English, meaning 'oaken'.

Airyck

Old Norse, from Eric, meaning 'eternal ruler'.

Ajani

African, meaning 'he fights for what he is'. Also Sanskrit, meaning 'of noble birth'.

A

Ajax

Greek, meaning 'mourner of the Earth'. Another Greek hero from the siege of Troy.

Ajay

Indian, meaning 'unconquerable'.

Ajit

Indian, meaning 'invincible'.

Akeem

Arabic, meaning 'wise or insightful'.

Akio

Japanese, meaning 'bright man'.

Akira

Japanese, meaning 'intelligent'.

Akiva

Hebrew, meaning 'to protect' or 'to shelter'.

Akon

American, made popular by the famous rapper charting in 2008/2009.

Aksel

Hebrew/Danish, meaning 'father of peace'.

Aladdin

Arabic, meaning 'servant of Allah'. Popular Disney character.

Alan

(alt. Allan, Allen, Allyn, Alun)

Gaelic, meaning 'rock'.

Alaric

Old German, meaning 'noble regal ruler'.

Alastair

(alt. Alasdair, Allister)

Greek/Gaelic, meaning 'defending men'.

Alban

Latin, meaning 'from Alba'. Also the Welsh and Scottish Gaelic word for 'Scotland'.

Alberic

Germanic, meaning 'Elfin king'.

Albert

Old German, meaning 'noble, bright, famous'.

A

Albin

Latin, meaning 'white'.

Albus

Latin, variant of Albin meaning 'white'. Also the first name of Albus Dumbledore, headmaster of Hogwarts School in the Harry Potter series.

Alcaeus

Greek, meaning 'strength'.

Alden

Old English, meaning 'old friend'.

Aldis

English, meaning 'from the old house'.

Aldo

Italian origin, meaning 'old' or 'elder'.

Aldric

English, meaning 'old King'.

Alec

(alt. Alek)

English, meaning 'defending men'.

Aled

Welsh, meaning 'child' or 'offspring'.

Alejandro

Spanish, meaning 'defender'. Made popular by Lady Gaga.

Alessio

Italian, meaning 'defender'.

Alexander

(alt. Alex, Alexandro, Alessandro)

Greek, meaning 'defending men'.

Alexei

Russian, meaning 'defender'.

Alfonso

Germanic/Spanish, meaning 'noble and prompt, ready to struggle'.

Alford

Old English, meaning 'old river/ford'.

Alfred

(alt. Alf, Alfi, Alfredo)

English, meaning 'elf' or 'magical counsel'.

Algernon

French, meaning 'with a moustache'.

Ali

(alt. Allie)

Arabic, meaning 'noble, sublime'.

Alijah

Hebrew, meaning 'the Lord is my God'.

Allison

English, meaning 'noble'.

Alois

German, meaning 'famous warrior'.

Alok

Indian, meaning 'cry of triumph'.

Alon

Jewish, meaning 'oak tree'.

Alonso

(alt. Alonzo)

Germanic, meaning 'noble and ready'.

Aloysius

Italian saint's name, meaning 'fame and war'.

A

Alpha

First letter of the Greek alphabet.

Alphaeus

Hebrew, meaning 'changing'.

Alpin

Gaelic, meaning 'related to the Alps'.

Altair

Arabic, meaning 'flying' or 'bird'.

Alter

Yiddish, meaning 'old man'.

Alton

Old English, meaning 'old town'.

Alva

Latin, meaning 'white'.

Alvie

German, meaning 'army of elves'.

A

Alvin
English, meaning 'friend of elves'.

Alwyn
Welsh, meaning 'wise friend'. May also come from the River Alwen in Wales.

Amachi
African, meaning 'who knows what God has brought us through this child'.

Amadeus
Latin, meaning 'God's love'.

Amadi
African, meaning 'appeared destined to die at birth'.

Amado
Spanish, meaning 'God's love'.

Amador
Spanish, meaning 'one who loves'.

Amari
Hebrew, meaning 'given by God'.

Amarion
Arabic, meaning 'populous, flushing'.

Amasa
Hebrew, meaning 'burden'.

Ambrose
Greek, meaning 'undying, immortal'.

Americo
Germanic, meaning 'ever powerful in battle'.

Amias
Latin, meaning 'loved'.

Amir
Hebrew, meaning 'prince' or 'treetop'.

Amit
Hindu, meaning 'friend'.

Ammon
Egyptian, meaning 'the hidden one'.

Amory
German/English, meaning 'work' and 'power'.

Amos

Hebrew, meaning 'encumbered' or 'burdened'.

Anacletus

Latin, meaning 'called back' or 'invoked'.

Anakin

American, meaning 'warrior'. Made famous by Anakin Skywalker in the Star Wars films.

Ananias

Greek/Italian, meaning 'answered by the Lord'.

Anastasius

Latin, meaning 'resurrection'.

Anat

Jewish, meaning 'water spring'.

Anatole

Greek, meaning 'cynical but without malice'.

Anders

Greek, meaning 'lion man'.

Anderson

English, meaning 'male'.

Andrew

(alt. Andreas, Andre, Andy)
Greek, meaning 'man' or 'warrior'.

Androcles

Greek, meaning 'glory of a warrior'.

Angel

Greek, meaning 'messenger'.

Angelo

Italian, meaning 'angel'.

Angus

Scottish, meaning 'one choice'.

Anil

Sanskrit, meaning 'air' or 'wind'.

Anselm

German, meaning 'helmet of God'.

Anson

English, meaning 'son of Agnes'.

Anthony

English, from the old Roman family name.

A

Antipas
Israeli, meaning 'for all or against all'.

Antwan
Old English, meaning 'flower'.

Apollo
Greek, meaning 'to destroy'. Greek god of the sun.

Apostolos
Greek, meaning 'apostle'.

Ara
Armenian. Ara was a legendary king.

Aragorn
Literary, used by Tolkien in *The Lord of the Rings* trilogy.

Aram
Hebrew, meaning 'Royal Highness'.

Aramis
Latin, meaning 'swordsman'.

Arcadio
Greek/Spanish, from a place in ancient Greece. The word 'Arcadia' (meaning paradise) comes from this.

Archibald
(alt.Archie)
Old German, meaning 'genuine/bold/brave'.

Ardell
Latin, meaning 'eager/burning with enthusiasm'.

Arden
Celtic, meaning 'high'.

Ares
Greek, meaning 'ruin'. Son of Zeus and Greek god of war.

Ari
Hebrew, meaning 'lion' or 'eagle'.

Arias
Germanic, meaning 'lion'.

Ariel
Hebrew, meaning 'lion of God'. One of the archangels, the angel of healing and new beginnings.

A

Arild
Old Norse, meaning 'battle commander'.

Aris
Greek, meaning 'best figure'.

Ariston
Greek, meaning 'the best'.

Aristotle
Greek, meaning 'best'. Also a famous philosopher.

Arjun
Sanskrit, meaning 'white'.

Arkady
Greek, region of central Greece.

Arlan
Gaelic, meaning 'pledge' or 'oath'.

Arlie
Old English place name, meaning 'eagle wood'.

Arlis
Hebrew, meaning 'pledge'.

Arlo
Spanish, meaning 'barberry tree'.

Armand
Old German, meaning 'soldier'.

Armani
Same origin as Armand meaning 'soldier', nowadays closely associated with the Italian designer.

Arnaldo
Spanish, meaning 'eagle power'.

Arnav
Indian, meaning 'the sea'.

Arnold
Old German, meaning 'eagle ruler'.

Arrow
English, from the common word denoting weaponry.

Art
Irish, name of a warrior in Irish mythology, Art Oenfer (Art the Lonely).

A

Arthur

(alt. Artie, Artis)

Celtic, probably from 'artos', meaning 'bear'. Made famous by the tales of King Arthur and the Knights of the Round Table.

Arturo

Celtic or Italian, meaning 'strong as a bear'.

Arvel

From the Welsh 'Arwel', meaning 'wept over'.

Arvid

English, meaning 'eagle in the woods'.

Arvind

Indian, meaning 'red lotus'.

Arvo

Finnish, meaning 'value' or 'worth'.

Arwen

Welsh, meaning 'fair' or 'fine'.

Asa

Hebrew, meaning 'doctor' or 'healer'.

Asante

African, meaning 'thank you'.

Asher

Hebrew, meaning 'fortunate' or 'lucky'.

Ashley

Old English, meaning 'ash meadow'.

Ashok

Sanskrit, meaning 'not causing sorrow'.

Ashton

English, meaning 'settlement in the ash-tree grove'.

Aslan

Turkish, meaning 'lion'. Strongly associated with the lion from C S Lewis's *The Lion, The Witch, and The Wardrobe*.

Asriel

Hebrew, meaning 'help of God'.

Astrophel

Latin, meaning 'star lover'.

A

Athanasios

Greek, meaning 'eternal life'.

Atílio

Portuguese, meaning 'father'.

Atlas

Greek, meaning 'to carry'. In Greek mythology Atlas was a Titan forced to carry the weight of the heavens.

Atlee

Hebrew, meaning 'God is just'.

Atticus

Latin, meaning 'from Athens'.

Auberon

Old German, meaning 'royal bear'.

Aubrey

Old German, meaning 'power'.

Auden

Old English, meaning 'old friend'.

Audie

Old English, meaning 'noble strength'.

August

Latin, meaning 'magnificent.

Literary names

Atticus (*To Kill A Mockingbird*, Harper Lee)
Cash (*As I Lay Dying*, William Faulkner)
Gatsby (*The Great Gatsby*, F. Scott Fitzgerald)
Holden (*The Catcher in the Rye*, J.D. Salinger)
Ishmael (*Moby Dick*, Herman Melville)
Rhett (*Gone With The Wind*, Margaret Mitchell)
Santiago (*Old Man and the Sea*, Ernest Hemingway)
Uncas (*The Last of the Mohicans*, James Fenimore Cooper)
Winfield (*The Grapes of Wrath*, John Steinbeck)
Yossarian (*Catch-22*, Joseph Heller)

A

Augustas
(alt. Augustus)
Latin, meaning 'venerated'.

Aurelien
French, meaning 'golden'.

Austin
Latin, meaning 'venerated'. Also a city in Texas.

Avi
Hebrew, meaning 'father of a multitude of nations'.

Awnan
Irish, meaning 'little Adam'.

Axel
Hebrew, meaning 'father is peace'. Made famous by Guns 'n' Roses frontman Axl Rose.

Azarel
Hebrew, meaning 'helped by God'.

Azaryah
Hebrew, meaning 'helped by God'.

Azriel
Hebrew, meaning 'God is my help'.

Azuko
African, meaning 'past glory'.

B

Boys' names

Babe

American, meaning 'baby'. Associated with baseball legend 'Babe' Ruth.

Baden

German, meaning 'battle'.

Bailey

English, meaning 'bailiff'.

Baird

Scottish, meaning 'poet' or 'one who sings ballads'.

Bakari

Swahili, meaning 'hope' or 'promise'.

Baker

English, from the word 'baker'.

Baldwin

Old French, meaning 'bold, brave friend'.

Balin

Old English. Balin was one of the Knights of the Round Table.

Balthazar

Babylonian, meaning 'protect the King'.

Balvinder

Hindu, meaning 'merciful, compassionate'.

Bannon

Irish, meaning descendant of O'Banain.

71

B

Barack

African, meaning 'blessed'. Made popular by the 44th President of the United States Barack Obama.

Barclay

Old English, meaning 'birch tree meadow'.

Barker

Old English, meaning 'shepherd'.

Barnaby

(alt. Barney)

Greek, meaning 'son of consolation'.

Barnard

English, meaning 'strong as a bear'.

Baron

Old English, meaning 'young warrior'.

Barrett

English, meaning 'strong as a bear'.

Barron

Old German, meaning 'old clearing'.

Barry

Irish Gaelic, meaning 'fair haired'.

Bart

(from Bartholomew)

Hebrew, meaning 'son of the farmer'. Made popular by the TV character Bart Simpson.

Barton

Old English, meaning 'barley settlement'.

Baruch

Hebrew, meaning 'blessed'.

Bascom

Old English, meaning 'from Bascombe'.

Bashir

Arabic, meaning 'well-educated' and 'wise'.

Basil

Greek, meaning 'royal, kingly'.

Basim

Arabic, meaning 'smile'.

B

Bastien

Greek, meaning 'revered'.

Baxter

Old English, meaning 'baker'.

Bayard

French, meaning 'auburn haired'.

Bayo

Nigerian, meaning 'to find joy'.

Baz

Irish Gaelic, meaning 'fair-haired'.

Beau

French, meaning 'handsome'.

Biblical names

David
John
Joseph
Luke
Mark
Matthew
Michael
Paul
Peter
Simon

Beck

Old Norse, meaning 'stream'.

Beckett

Old English, meaning 'beehive' or 'bee cottage'. Associated with the Irish writer Samuel Beckett.

Beckham

English, meaning 'homestead by the stream'. Made famous by English Soccer star David Beckham.

Béla

Hungarian, meaning 'within'.

Belarius

Shakespearean, meaning 'a banished lord'.

Benedict

Latin, meaning 'blessed'.

Benjamin

(alt. Ben)

Hebrew, meaning 'son of the south'.

Bennett

French/Latin vernacular form of Benedict, meaning 'blessed'.

B

Benoit
French form of Benedict, meaning 'blessed'.

Benson
English, meaning 'son of Ben'.

Bentley
Old English, meaning 'bent grass meadow'.

Benton
Old English, meaning 'town in the bent grass'.

Beriah
Hebrew, meaning 'in fellowship' or 'in envy'.

Bernard
(alt. Bernie)
Germanic, meaning 'strong, brave bear'.

Berry
Old English, meaning 'berry'.

Bert
(alt. Bertram, Bertrand)
Old English, meaning 'illustrious'.

Berton
Old English, meaning 'bright settlement'.

Bevan
Welsh, meaning 'son of Evan'.

Bicknell
Old English, meaning 'from Bicknell'.

Bilal
Arabic, meaning 'wetting, refreshing'.

Bill
(alt. Billy)
English, from William, meaning 'determined' or 'resolute'.

Birch
Old English, meaning 'bright' or 'shining'.

Birger
Norwegian, meaning 'rescue'.

Bishop
Old English, meaning 'bishop'.

Bjorn
Old Norse, meaning 'bear'.

Bladen

Hebrew, meaning 'hero'.

Blaine

Irish Gaelic, meaning 'yellow'.

Blair

English, meaning 'plain'.

Blaise

French, meaning 'lisp' or 'stutter'.

Blake

Old English, meaning 'dark, black'.

Blas

(alt. Blaze)

German, meaning 'firebrand'.

Bo

Scandinavian, short form of Robert, meaning 'bright fame'.

Boaz

Hebrew, meaning 'swiftness' or 'strength'.

Bob

(alt. Bobby)

From Robert, Old German meaning 'bright fame'.

B

Boden

(alt. Bodie)

Scandinavian, meaning 'shelter'.

Bogumil

Slavic, meaning 'God's favor'.

Bond

Old English, meaning 'peasant farmer'.

Boris

Slavic, meaning 'battle glory'.

Bosten

English, meaning 'town by the woods'.

Bowen

Welsh, meaning 'son of Owen'.

Boyd

Scottish Gaelic, meaning 'yellow'.

Brad

(alt. Bradley)

Old English, meaning 'broad' or 'wide'.

B

Saints' names

Anselm
Bartholomew
Francis
Gabriel
Gregory
Jerome
Nicholas
Philip
Stephen
Thomas

Brady

Irish, meaning 'large-chested'.

Bradyn
(alt. Braden, Bradan)

Gaelic, meaning 'descendant of Bradan'.

Bram

Gaelic, meaning 'raven'.

Brando

Old Norse, meaning 'sword' or 'flaming torch'. Associated with movie star Marlon Brando.

Brandon

Old English, meaning 'gorse'.

Brandt

Old English, meaning 'beacon'.

Brannon

Gaelic, meaning 'raven'.

Branson

English, meaning 'son of Brand'.

Brant

Old English, meaning 'hill'.

Braulio

Greek, meaning 'shining'.

Brendan

Gaelic, meaning 'prince'.

Brennan

Gaelic, meaning 'teardrop'.

Brenton

English, from Brent, meaning 'hill'.

Brett

English, meaning 'a Breton'.

B

Brian

Gaelic, meaning 'high' or 'noble'.

Brice

Latin, meaning 'speckled'.

Brier

French, meaning 'heather'.

Brock

Old English, meaning 'badger'.

Broderick

English, meaning 'ruler'.

Brody

Gaelic, meaning both 'ditch' and 'brother'.

Brogan

Irish, meaning 'sturdy shoe'.

Bronwyn

Welsh, meaning 'white breasted'.

Brook

English, meaning 'stream'.

Bruce

Scottish, meaning 'high' or 'noble'.

Bruno

Germanic, meaning 'brown'.

Bryant

English variant of Brian, meaning 'high' or 'noble'.

Bryce

Scottish, meaning 'of Britain'.

Brycen

Scottish, meaning 'son of Bryce'.

Bryden

Irish, meaning 'strong one'.

Bryson

Welsh, meaning 'descendant of Brice'.

Bubba

American, meaning 'boy'.

Buck

American, meaning 'goat' or 'deer'.

B

Bud
(alt. Buddy)
American, meaning 'friend'.

Burdett
Middle English, meaning 'bird'.

Burke
French, meaning 'fortified settlement'.

Burl
French, meaning 'knotty wood'.

Buzz
American, shortened form of Busby, meaning 'village in the thicket'. Associated with the astronaut Buzz Aldrin.

Byron
Old English, meaning 'barn'. Made famous by the poet Lord Byron.

C

Boys' names

Cabot
Old English, meaning 'to sail'.

Cade
(alt. Caden)
English, meaning 'round, lumpy'.

Cadence
Latin, meaning 'with rhythm'.

Cadogan
Welsh, meaning 'battle glory and honor'.

Caedmon
Celtic, meaning 'wise warrior'.

Caelan
Gaelic, from St Columba.

Caerwyn
(alt. Carwyn, Gerwyn)
Welsh, meaning 'white fort' or 'settlement'.

Caesar
(alt. Cesar)
Latin, meaning 'head of hair'. Made famous by the first Roman emperor Julius Caesar.

Caetano
Portuguese, meaning 'from Gaeta, Italy'

Caiden
Arabic, meaning 'companion'.

Caillou
French, meaning 'pebble'.

C

Cain
Hebrew, brother of Abel.

Cainan
Hebrew, meaning 'possessor' or 'purchaser'.

Cairo
Egyptian city.

Cal
Short form of names beginning Cal-.

Calder
Scottish, meaning 'rough waters'.

Caleb
Hebrew, meaning 'dog'.

Calen
From Caleb, meaning 'dog'.

Calix
Greek, meaning 'very handsome'.

Callahan
Irish, meaning 'contention' or 'strife'.

Callum
Gaelic, meaning 'dove'.

Calvin
French, meaning 'little bald one'.

Camden
Gaelic, meaning 'winding valley'.

Cameron
Scottish Gaelic, meaning 'crooked nose'.

Camillo
Latin, meaning 'free born' or 'noble'.

Campbell
Scottish Gaelic, meaning 'crooked mouth'.

Canaan
Hebrew, meaning 'to be humbled'.

Candido
Latin, meaning 'candid' or 'honest'.

C

Cannon

French, meaning 'of the church'.

Canton

French, 'dweller of corner'. Also name given to areas of Switzerland.

Cappy

Italian, meaning 'lucky'.

Carden

Old English, meaning 'wood carder'.

Carey

Gaelic, meaning 'love'.

Carl

Old Norse, meaning 'free man'.

Carlo

Italian form of Carl, meaning 'free man'.

Carlos

Spanish form of Carl, meaning 'free man'.

Carlton

Old English, meaning 'free peasant settlement'.

Carmelo

Latin, meaning 'garden' or 'orchard'.

Carmen

Latin/Spanish, meaning 'song'.

Carmine

Latin, meaning 'song'.

Carnell

English, meaning 'defender of the castle'.

Carson

(alt. Carsten)

Scottish, meaning 'marsh-dwellers'.

Carter

Old English, meaning 'transporter of goods'.

Cary

Old Celtic river name. Also means 'love'.

Case

(alt. Casey)

Irish Gaelic, meaning 'alert' or 'watchful'.

C

Cash

Latin, shortened form of Cassius, meaning 'empty, hollow'.

Casimer

Slavic, meaning 'famous destroyer of peace'.

Cason

Latin, from Cassius, meaning 'empty' or 'hollow'.

Casper

Persian, meaning 'treasurer'.

Caspian

English, meaning 'of the Caspy people'. From the Caspian Sea.

Cassidy

Gaelic, meaning 'curly haired'.

Cassius

(alt. Cassio)

Latin, meaning 'empty, hollow'.

Cathal

Celtic, meaning 'battle rule'.

Cato

Latin, meaning 'all-knowing'.

Cecil

Latin, meaning 'blind'.

Cedar

English, name of an evergreen tree.

TV personality names

Billy (Bush)	Mario (Lopez)
Conon (O'Brien)	Nick (Cannon)
Jay (Leno)	Ryan (Seacrest)
Jeff (Probst)	Stephen (Colbert)
Jon (Stewart)	Tom (Bergeron)

C

Cedric

Welsh, meaning 'spectacular bounty'.

Celestino

Spanish/Italian meaning 'heavenly'.

Chad

(alt. Chadrick)

Old English, meaning 'warlike, warrior'.

Chaim

Hebrew, meaning 'life'.

Champion

English, from the word 'champion'.

Chance

English, from the word 'chance, meaning 'good fortune'.

Chandler

Old English, meaning 'candle maker and seller'.

Charles

(alt. Charlie)

Old German, meaning 'free man'.

Chase

Old French, meaning 'huntermen'.

Chaska

Native American name usually given to first son.

Che

Spanish, shortened form of José. Made famous by Che Guevara.

Chesley

Old English, meaning 'camp on the meadow'.

Chester

Latin, meaning 'camp of soldiers'.

Chima

Old English, meaning 'hilly land'.

Christian

English, from the word 'Christian'.

Christophe

French variant of Christopher, meaning 'bearing Christ inside'.

C

Christopher

Greek, meaning 'bearing Christ inside'.

Cian

Irish, meaning 'ancient'.

Ciaran

Irish, meaning 'black'.

Cicero

Latin, meaning 'chickpea'. Also a famous Roman philosopher and orator.

Cimarron

City in western Kansas.

Ciprian

Latin, meaning 'from Cyprus'.

Ciro

Spanish, meaning 'sun'.

Clancy

Old Irish, meaning 'red warrior'.

Clarence

Latin, meaning 'one who lives near the river Clare'.

Clark

Latin, meaning 'clerk'.

Claude

(alt. Claudie, Claudio, Claudius)
Latin, meaning 'lame'.

Claus

Variant of Nicholas, meaning 'people of victory'.

Clay

English, from the word 'clay'.

Clement

(alt. Clem)
Latin, meaning 'merciful'.

Cleo

Greek, meaning 'glory'.

Cletus

Greek, meaning 'illustrious'.

Cliff

(alt. Clifford, Clifton)
English, from the word 'cliff'.

Clint

(alt. Clinton)
Old English, meaning 'fenced settlement'.

Clive

Old English, meaning 'cliff' or 'slope'.

Clyde

Scottish, from the river in Glasgow.

Coby

(alt. Cody, Colby)

Irish, son of Oda.

Colden

Old English, meaning 'dark valley'.

Cole

Old French, meaning 'coal black'.

Coley

Old English, meaning 'coal black'.

Colin

Gaelic, meaning 'young creature'.

Colson

Old English, meaning 'coal black'.

Colton

English, meaning 'swarthy'.

Columbus

Latin, meaning 'dove'.

Colwyn

Welsh, from the river in Wales.

Conan

Gaelic, meaning 'wolf'.

Conley

Gaelic, meaning 'sensible'.

Connell

(alt. Connolly)

Irish, meaning 'high' or 'mighty'.

Connor

(alt. Conrad, Conroy)

Irish, meaning 'lover of hounds'.

Constant

(alt. Constantine)

English, from the word 'constant'.

Cooper

Old English, meaning 'barrel maker'.

C

C

Corban

Hebrew, meaning 'dedicated and belonging to God'.

Corbett
(alt. Corbin, Corby)

Norman French, meaning 'young crow'.

Cordell

Old English, meaning 'cord maker'.

Corey

Gaelic, meaning 'hill hollow'.

Corin

Latin, meaning 'spear'.

Cormac

Gaelic, meaning 'impure son'.

Cornelius
(alt. Cornell)

Latin, meaning 'horn'.

Cortez

Spanish, meaning 'courteous'.

Corwin

Old English, meaning 'heart's friend' or 'companion'.

Cosimo
(alt. Cosme, Cosmo)

Italian, meaning 'order' or 'beauty'.

Coty

French, meaning 'riverbank'.

Coulter

English, meaning 'young horse'.

Courtney

Old English, meaning 'domain of Curtis'.

Uncommon three syllable names

Alastair
Barnaby
Dominic
Elijah
Elliot
Gideon
Nathaniel
Reginald
Theodore

C

Cowan
Gaelic, meaning 'hollow in the hill'.

Craig
Welsh, meaning 'rock'.

Crispin
Latin, meaning 'curly haired'.

Croix
French, meaning 'cross'.

Cruz
Spanish, meaning 'cross'.

Curran
Gaelic, meaning 'dagger' or 'hero'.

Curtis
(alt. Curt)
Old French, meaning 'courteous'.

Cutler
Old English, meaning 'knife maker'.

Cyprian
English, meaning 'from Cyprus'.

Cyril
Greek, meaning 'master' or 'Lord'.

Cyrus
Persian, meaning 'Lord'.

Popular American names for boys and girls

Aubree	Kendra
Brayden	Lacey
Cooper	Landon
Grayson	Misty
Kayla	Peyton

87

C

Popular names of English and Scottish Kings and Consorts

Alexander	James
Charles	Richard
Edward	Robert
George	Stephen
Henry	William

D Boys' names

Dafydd
Welsh, meaning 'beloved'.

Daichi
Japanese, meaning 'great wisdom'.

Daisuke
Japanese, meaning 'lionhearted'.

Dakari
African, meaning 'happy'.

Dakota
Native American, meaning 'friend' or 'ally'.

Dale
Old English, meaning 'valley'.

Dallin
English, meaning 'dweller in the valley'.

Dalton
English, meaning 'town in the valley'.

Daly
Gaelic, meaning 'assembly'.

Damarion
Greek, meaning 'gentle'.

Damian
(alt. Damon)
Greek, meaning 'to tame, subdue'.

D

Dane

Old English, meaning 'from Denmark'.

Daniel

(alt. Dan, Danny)

Hebrew, meaning 'God is my judge'.

Dante

Latin, meaning 'lasting'. Associated with the famous Italian 13th century poet Dante Alighieri.

Darby

Irish, meaning 'without envy'.

Darcy

Gaelic, meaning 'dark'. Associated with Jane Austen's Mr Darcy.

Dario

(alt. Darius)

Greek, meaning 'Kingly'.

Darnell

Old English, meaning 'the hidden spot'.

Darragh

Irish, meaning 'dark oak'.

Darrell

(alt. Daryl)

Old English, meaning 'open'.

Darren

(alt. Darrian)

Gaelic, meaning 'great'.

Darrick

Old German, meaning 'power of the tribe'.

Darshan

Hindi, meaning 'vision'.

Darwin

Old English, meaning 'dear friend'.

Dash

(alt. Dashawn)

American, meaning 'enlightened one'.

Dashiell

French, meaning 'page boy'.

David

(alt. Dave, Davey, Davie, Davian)

Hebrew, meaning 'beloved'.

D

Davis

Old English, meaning 'son of David'.

Dawson

Old English, meaning 'son of David'.

Dax

(alt. Daxton)

French, from the town in southwestern France.

Dayal

Indian, meaning 'kind'.

Dayton

Old English, meaning 'David's place'.

Dean

Old English, meaning 'valley'.

Declan

Irish, meaning 'full of goodness'.

Dedric

Old English, meaning 'gifted ruler'.

Deegan

(alt. Deagon, Daegan)

Irish, meaning 'black-haired'.

Deepak

(alt. Deepan)

Indian, meaning 'illumination'.

Del

(alt. Delano, Delbert, Dell)

Old English, meaning 'bright shining one'.

Demetrius

Greek, meaning 'harvest lover'.

Dempsey

Irish, meaning 'proud'.

Denham

(alt. Denholm)

Old English, meaning 'valley settlement'.

Dennis

(alt. Denny, Denton)

English, meaning 'follower of Dionysius'.

Denver

Old English, meaning 'green valley'. City in Colorado.

D

Old name, new fashion?

Augustus
Bertrand
Edgar
Felix
Gilbert
Hector
Jasper
Norris
Percival
Reginald
Sebastian
Theodore
Winston

Denzil

English, meaning 'fort'. Also a town in Cornwall, England.

Deon

Greek, meaning 'of Zeus'.

Derek

English, meaning 'power of the tribe'.

Dermot

Irish, meaning 'free man'.

Desmond

Irish, meaning 'from south Munster'.

Destin

French, meaning 'destiny'.

Devyn

Irish, meaning 'poet'.

Dewey

Welsh, from Dewi (David).

Dexter

(alt. Dex)

Latin, meaning 'right-handed'.

Dick

(alt. Dickie, Dickon)

From Richard, meaning 'powerful leader'.

Didier

French, meaning 'much desired'.

Diego

Spanish, meaning 'supplanter'.

Dietrich

Old German, meaning 'power of the tribe'.

D

Diggory
English, meaning 'dyke'.

Dilbert
English, meaning 'day-bright'.

Dimitri
(alt. Dimitrios, Dimitris)
Greek, meaning 'Prince'.

Dino
Diminutive of Dean, meaning 'valley'.

Dion
Greek, short form of Dionysius.

Dirk
Variant of Derek, meaning 'power of the tribe'.

Dobbin
Diminutive of Robert, meaning 'bright fame'.

Dominic
Latin, meaning 'Lord'.

Donald
(alt. Don, Donal, Donaldo)
Gaelic, meaning 'great chief'.

Donato
Italian, meaning 'gift'.

Donnell
(alt. Donnie, Donny)
Gaelic, meaning 'world fighter'.

Donovan
Gaelic, meaning 'dark-haired chief'.

Doran
Gaelic, meaning 'exile'.

Dorian
Greek, meaning 'descendant of Doris'.

Douglas
(alt. Dougal, Dougie)
Scottish, meaning 'black river'.

Draco
Latin, meaning 'dragon'. Made popular by the character Draco Malfoy in the Harry Potter series.

Drake
Greek, meaning 'dragon'.

D

Drew

Shortened form of Andrew, Greek, meaning 'man' or 'warrior'.

Dudley

Old English, meaning 'people's field'.

Duff

Gaelic, meaning 'swarthy'.

Duke

Latin, meaning 'leader'.

Duncan

Scottish, meaning 'dark warrior'.

Dustin

(alt. Dusty)

French, meaning 'brave warrior'.

Dwayne

Irish Gaelic, meaning 'swarthy'.

Dwight

Flemish, meaning 'blond'.

Dwyer

Gaelic, meaning 'dark wise one'.

Dylan

(alt. Dillon)

Welsh, meaning 'son of the sea'.

E Boys' names

Eamon
(alt. Eames)
Irish, meaning 'wealthy protector'.

Earl
(alt. Earle, Errol)
English, meaning 'nobleman, warrior'.

Ebb
Shortened form of Ebenezer, meaning 'stone of help'.

Ebenezer
Hebrew, meaning 'stone of help'.

Ed
(alt. Edd, Eddie, Eddy)
Shortened form of Edward, Old English, meaning 'wealthy guard'.

Edgar
(alt. Elgar)
Old English, meaning 'wealthy spear'.

Edison
English, meaning 'son of Edward'.

Edmund
English, meaning 'wealthy protector'.

Edric
Old English, meaning 'rich and powerful'.

Edsel
Old German, meaning 'noble'.

E

Edward
(alt. Eduardo)
Old English, meaning 'wealthy guard'.

Edwin
English, meaning 'wealthy friend'.

Efrain
Hebrew, meaning 'fruitful'.

Egan
Irish, meaning 'fire'.

Einar
Old Norse, meaning 'battle leader'.

Eladio
Greek, meaning 'Greek'.

Elam
Hebrew, meaning 'eternal'.

Elbert
Old English, meaning 'famous'.

Eldon
Old English, meaning 'Ella's hill'.

Eldred
(alt. Eldridge)
Old English, meaning 'old venerable counsel'.

Elgin
Old English, meaning 'high minded'.

Eli
(alt. Eliah)
Hebrew, meaning 'high'.

Elias
(alt. Elijah)
Hebrew, meaning 'the Lord is my God'.

Elio
Spanish, meaning 'the Lord is my God'.

Ellery
Old English, meaning 'elder tree'.

Elliott
Variant of Elio. Spanish, meaning 'the Lord is my God'.

Ellis
Welsh variant of Elio, meaning 'the Lord is my God'.

E

Ellison

English, meaning 'son of Ellis'.

Elmer

(alt. Elmo)

Old English, meaning 'noble'; Arabic, meaning 'aristocratic'.

Elon

Hebrew, meaning 'oak tree'.

Elroy

French, meaning 'king'.

Elton

Old English, meaning 'Ella's town'.

Elvin

English, meaning 'elf-like'.

Elvis

Figure in Norse mythology. Made famous by the singer Elvis Presley.

Emanuel

Hebrew, meaning 'God is with us'.

Emeric

German, meaning 'work rule'.

Emile

(alt. Emiliano, Emilio)

Latin, meaning 'eager'.

Emlyn

Welsh, name of town in West Wales, UK.

Emmett

English, meaning 'universal'.

Emrys

Welsh, meaning 'immortal'.

Enoch

Hebrew, meaning 'dedicated'.

Enrico

(alt. Enrique)

Italian form of Henry, meaning 'home ruler'.

Enzo

Italian, short for Lorenzo, meaning 'laurel'.

Eoghan

(alt. Eoin)

Irish form of Owen, meaning 'well born' or 'noble'.

E

Ephron
(alt. Effron)
Hebrew, meaning 'dust'.

Erasmo
(alt. Erasmus)
Greek, meaning 'to love'.

Eric
Old Norse, meaning 'ruler'.

Ernest
(alt. Ernesto, Ernie, Ernst)
Old German, meaning 'serious'.

Erskine
Scottish, meaning 'high cliff'.

Erwin
Old English, meaning 'boar friend'.

Ethan
(alt. Etienne)
Hebrew, meaning 'long lived'.

Eugene
Greek, meaning 'well born'.

Evan
Welsh, meaning 'God is good'.

Everard
Old English, meaning 'strong boar'.

Everett
English, meaning 'strong boar'.

Ewald
(alt. Ewan, Ewell)
Old English, from Owen, meaning 'well born' or 'noble'.

Ezra
Hebrew, meaning 'helper'.

F

Boys' names

Fabian
(alt. *Fabien, Fabio*)
Latin, meaning 'one who grows beans'.

Fabrice
(alt. *Fabrizio*)
Latin, meaning 'works with his hands'.

Faisal
Arabic, meaning 'resolute'.

Faron
Spanish, meaning 'pharaoh'.

Farrell
Gaelic, meaning 'hero'.

Faulkner
Latin, from 'falcon'.

Faustino
Latin, meaning 'fortunate'.

Felix
(alt. *Felice*)
Italian/Latin, meaning 'happy'.

Felipe
(alt. *Filippo*)
Spanish, meaning 'lover of horses'.

Fennel
Latin, name of a herb.

F

Names of poets

Alfred (Lord Tennyson)
Allen (Ginsberg)
Dylan (Thomas)
Geoffrey (Chaucer)
Kingsley (Amis)

Langston (Hughes)
Ralph (Waldo Emerson)
Robert (Burns)
Seamus (Heaney)
William (Wordsworth)

Ferdinand
(alt. Fernando)
Old German, meaning 'bold voyager'.

Fergus
(alt. Ferguson)
Gaelic, meaning 'supreme man'.

Ferris
Gaelic, meaning 'rock'.

Fidel
Latin, meaning 'faithful'.

Finbar
Gaelic, meaning 'fair head'.

Finian
Gaelic, meaning 'fair'.

Finlay
(alt. Finley, Finn)
Gaelic, meaning 'fair-haired courageous one'.

Finnegan
Gaelic, meaning 'fair'.

Fintan
Gaelic, meaning 'little fair one'.

Flavio
Latin, meaning 'yellow hair'.

F

Florencio
(alt. Florentino)

Latin, meaning 'from Florence'.

Florian
(alt. Florin)

Slavic/Latin, meaning 'flower'.

Floyd

Welsh, meaning 'gray haired'.

Flynn

Gaelic, meaning 'with a ruddy complexion'.

Fortunato

Italian, meaning 'lucky'.

Forrest
(alt. Forest)

Old French, meaning 'woodsman'. Made popular by the movie *Forrest Gump*.

Foster

Old English, meaning 'woodsman'.

Fotini
(alt. Fotis)

Greek, meaning 'light'.

Francesco
(alt. Francis, Francisco, Franco, François)

Latin, meaning 'from France'.

Frank
(alt. Frankie, Franklin, Franz)

Middle English, meaning 'free landholder'.

Fraser

Scottish, meaning 'of the forest men'.

Fred
(alt. Freddie, Frederick)

Old German, meaning 'peaceful ruler'.

Furman

Old German, meaning 'ferryman'.

Popular African names for boys and girls

Abiba	Jelani
Chike	Kanene
Ebere	Keisha
Faizah	Razi
Fola	Salim

G Boys' names

G

Gabe

Hebrew, shortened form of Gabriel, meaning 'hero of God'.

Gabino

Latin, meaning 'God is my strength'.

Gabriel

Hebrew, meaning 'hero of God'.

Gael

English, old reference to the Celts.

Gage

(alt. Gaige)

Old French, meaning 'pledge'.

Galen

Greek, meaning 'healer'.

Galileo

Italian, meaning 'from Galilee'.

Ganesh

Hindi, meaning 'Lord of the throngs'. One of the Hindu deities.

Gannon

Irish, meaning 'fair skinned'.

Gareth

(alt. Garth)

Welsh, meaning 'gentle'.

Garfield

Old English, meaning 'spear field'. Also the name of the cartoon cat.

103

G

Garland

English, as in 'garland of flowers'.

Garnet

English, precious stone red in color.

Garrett

(alt. Garet)

Germanic, meaning 'strength of the spear'.

Gary

(alt. Garry, Geary)

Old English, meaning 'spear'.

Gaspar

(alt. Gaspard)

Persian, meaning 'treasurer'.

Gaston

From the region in the south of France.

Gavin

(alt. Gawain)

Scottish/Welsh, meaning 'little falcon'.

Gene

Greek, shortened form of Eugene, meaning 'well born'.

Gennaro

Italian, meaning 'of Janus'.

Geoffrey

Old German, meaning 'peace'.

George

(alt. Giorgio)

Greek, meaning 'farmer'.

Gerald

(alt. Geraldo, Gerard, Gerardo, Gerhard)

Old German, meaning 'spear ruler'.

Geronimo

Italian, meaning 'sacred name'.

Gerry

English, meaning 'independent'.

Gert

Old German, meaning 'strong spear'.

Gervase

Old German, meaning 'with honor'.

G

Giacomo
Italian, meaning 'God's son'.

Gibson
English, meaning 'son of Gilbert'.

Gideon
Hebrew, meaning 'tree cutter'.

Gilbert
(alt. Gilberto)
French, meaning 'bright promise'.

Giles
Greek, meaning 'small goat'.

Gino
Italian, meaning 'well born'.

Giovanni
Italian form of John, meaning 'God is gracious'.

Giulio
Italian, meaning 'youthful'.

Giuseppe
Italian form of Joseph, meaning 'Jehovah increases'.

Glen
(alt. Glyn)
English, from the word 'glen'.

Godfrey
German, meaning 'peace of God'.

Gordon
Gaelic, meaning 'large fortification'.

Gottlieb
German, meaning 'good love'.

Graeme
(alt. Graham)
English, meaning 'gravelled area'.

Names from ancient Rome

Brutus
Caesar
Julius
Lucius
Marcus
Maximus
Nero
Rufus
Titus

G

Grant
English, from the word 'grant'.

Granville
English, meaning 'gravelly town'.

Gray
(alt. Grey)
English, from the word 'gray'.

Grayson
English, meaning 'son of gray'.

Green
English, from the word 'green'.

Greg
(alt. Gregorio, Gregory, Grieg)
English, meaning 'watcher'.

Griffin
English, from the word 'griffin'.

Guido
Italian, meaning 'guide'.

Guillaume
French form of William, meaning 'strong protector'.

Gulliver
English, meaning 'glutton'.

Gunther
German, meaning 'warrior'.

Gurpreet
Indian, meaning 'love of the teacher'.

Gustave
(alt. Gus)
Scandinavian, meaning 'royal staff'.

Guy
English, from the word 'guy'.

Gwyn
Welsh, meaning 'white'.

H

Boys' names

Habib
Arabic, meaning 'beloved one'.

Haden
(alt. Haiden)
English, meaning 'hedged valley'.

Hades
Greek, meaning 'sightless'. Name of the underworld in Greek mythology.

Hadrian
From Hadria, a north Italian city.

Hadwin
Old English, meaning 'friend in war'.

Hakeem
Arabic, meaning 'wise and insightful'.

Hal
(alt. Hale, Hallie)
English, nickname for Henry, meaning 'home ruler'.

Hamid
Arabic, meaning 'praiseworthy'.

Hamilton
Old English, meaning 'flat topped hill'.

Hamish
Scottish form of James, meaning 'he who supplants'.

H

Hampus
Swedish form of Homer, meaning 'pledge'.

Hamza
Arabic, meaning 'lamb'.

Han
(alt. Hannes, Hans)
Scandinavian, meaning 'the Lord is gracious'.

Hank
German, meaning 'home ruler'. Form of Henry.

Hansel
German, meaning 'the Lord is gracious'.

Hardy
English, meaning 'tough'.

Harlan
English, meaning 'dweller by the boundary wood'.

Harland
Old English, meaning 'army land'.

Harley
Old English, meaning 'hare meadow'.

Harmon
Old German, meaning 'soldier'.

Harold
Scandinavian, meaning 'army ruler'.

Harry
Old German, meaning 'home ruler'. Form of Henry.

Hart
Old English, meaning 'stag'.

Names from ancient Greece

Aesop
Demetrius
Erasmus
Georgios
Homer
Jason
Lysandos
Nikolaos
Pyrrhus
Theodore

H

Harvey
Old English, meaning 'strong and worthy'.

Haskell
Hebrew, meaning 'intellect'.

Hassan
Arabic, meaning 'handsome'.

Haydn
(alt. Hayden)
Old English, meaning 'hedged valley'.

Heart
English, from the word 'heart'.

Heath
English, meaning 'heath' or 'moor'.

Heathcliff
English, meaning 'cliff near a heath'. Made famous by Emily Bronte's novel *Wuthering Heights*.

Heber
Hebrew, meaning 'partner'.

Hector
Greek, meaning 'steadfast'.

Henry
(alt. Henri, Hendrik, Hendrix)
Old German, meaning 'home ruler'.

Henson
English, meaning 'son of Henry'.

Herbert
(alt. Bert, Herb, Heriberto)
Old German, meaning 'illustrious warrior'.

Herman
(alt. Herminio, Hermon)
Old German, meaning 'soldier'.

Hermes
Greek, meaning 'messenger'.

Herschel
Yiddish, meaning 'deer'.

Hezekiah
Hebrew, meaning 'God gives strength'.

H

Hideki

Japanese, meaning 'excellent trees'.

Hideo

Japanese, meaning 'excellent name'.

Hilario

Latin, meaning 'cheerful, happy'.

Hilary

English, meaning 'cheerful'.

Hillel

Hebrew, meaning 'greatly praised'.

Hilliard

Old German, meaning 'battle guard'.

Hilton

Old English, meaning 'hill settlement'.

Hiram

Hebrew, meaning 'exalted brother'.

Hiro

Spanish, meaning 'sacred name'.

Hiroshi

Japanese, meaning 'generous'.

Hirsch

Yiddish, meaning 'deer'.

Hobart

English, meaning 'bright and shining intellect'.

Hodge

English, meaning 'son of Roger'.

Hogan

Gaelic, meaning 'youth'.

Holden

English, meaning 'deep valley'.

Hollis

Old English, meaning 'holly tree'.

Homer

Greek, meaning 'pledge'.

H

Honorius

Latin, meaning 'honorable'.

Horace

Latin, name of the Roman poet.

Houston

Old English, meaning 'Hugh's town'.

Howard

Old English, meaning 'noble watchman'.

Howell

Welsh, meaning 'eminent and remarkable'.

Hoyt

Norse, meaning 'spirit' or 'soul'.

Hristo

From Christo, meaning 'follower of Christ'.

Hubert

German, meaning 'bright and shining intellect'.

Hudson

Old English, meaning 'son of Hugh'.

Hugh

(alt. Huw)

Old German, meaning 'soul, mind and intellect'.

Humbert

Old German, meaning 'famous giant'. Made famous by the paedophile protagonist of Vladimir Nabokov's *Lolita*.

Humphrey

Old German, meaning 'peaceful warrior'.

Hunter

English, from the word 'hunter'.

Hurley

Gaelic, meaning 'sea tide'.

Huxley

Old English, meaning 'Hugh's meadow'.

Hyrum

Hebrew, meaning 'exalted brother'.

H

Names with positive meanings

Auden – Friend

Basim – Smile

Dustin – Brave

Ervin – Beautiful

Gene – Noble

Jamal – Handsome

Jay – Happy

Lucas – Light

Tate – Cheerful

Tova – Good

I
Boys' names

Iago

Spanish, meaning 'he who supplants'.

Ian
(alt. Ion)

Gaelic, variant of John, meaning 'God is gracious'.

Ianto

Welsh, meaning 'gift of God'.

Ibrahim

Arabic, meaning 'father of many'.

Ichabod

Hebrew, meaning 'glory is good'.

Ichiro

Japanese, meaning 'firstborn son'.

Girls' names for boys (male spellings)

Casey
Darcy
Gene
Kay
Kelly
Kelsey
Madison
Nat
Sandy
Sasha

I

Idris

Welsh, meaning 'fiery leader'.

Ifan

Welsh variant of John, meaning 'God is gracious'.

Ignacio

Latin, meaning 'ardent' or 'burning'.

Ignatz

German, meaning 'fiery'.

Igor

Russian, meaning 'Ing's soldier'.

Ikaika

Hawaiian, meaning 'strong'.

Ike

Hebrew, short for Isaac, meaning 'laughter'.

Ilan

Hebrew, meaning 'tree'.

Ilias

Variant of Elijah. Hebrew, meaning 'the Lord is my God'.

Imanol

Hebrew, meaning 'God is with us'.

Indiana

Latin, meaning 'from India'.

Indigo

English, describing a deep blue color.

Ingo

Danish, meaning 'meadow'.

Inigo

Spanish, meaning 'fiery'.

Ioannis

Greek, meaning 'the Lord is gracious'.

Ira

Hebrew, meaning 'full grown and watchful'.

Irvin
(alt. Irving, Irwin)

Gaelic, meaning 'green and fresh water'.

I

Isaac
(alt. Isaak)
Hebrew, meaning 'laughter'.

Isadore
(alt. Isidore, Isidro)
Greek, meaning 'gift of Isis'.

Isai
(alt. Isaiah, Isaias, Izaiah)
Arabic, meaning 'protection and security'.

Iser
Yiddish, meaning 'God wrestler'.

Ishmael
(alt. Ismael)
Hebrew, meaning 'God listens'.

Israel
Hebrew, meaning 'God perseveres'. Also the name of the country.

Istvan
Hungarian variant of Stephen, meaning 'crowned'.

Place names

Adrian
Austin
Bradley
Brooklyn
Cheyenne
Dallas
Glen
Houston
Paris
Tay

Itai
Hebrew, meaning 'the Lord is with me'.

Ivan
Hebrew, meaning 'God is gracious'.

Ivanhoe
Russian origin, meaning 'God is gracious'. Also name of the novel by Walter Scott.

Ivey
English, variant of Ivy.

I

Ivo

From the French 'yves', meaning 'yew tree'.

Ivor

Scandinavian, meaning 'yew'.

Ivory

English, from the word 'ivory'.

Long names

Alexander
Bartholomew
Christopher
Demetrius
Giovanni
Maximillian
Montgomery
Nathaniel
Sebastian
Zachariah

J

Boys' names

Jabari
Swahili, meaning 'valiant'.

Jabez
Hebrew, meaning 'borne in pain'.

Jace
(alt. Jaece, Jase, Jayce)
Hebrew, meaning 'healer'.

Jacek
(alt. Jacirto)
African, meaning 'hyacinth'.

Jack
(alt. Jackie, Jacky)
From the Hebrew John, meaning 'God is gracious'.

Jackson
(alt. Jaxon)
English, meaning 'son of Jack'.

Jacob
(alt. Jaco, Jacobo, Jago)
Hebrew, meaning 'he who supplants'.

Jacques
French form of Jack, meaning 'God is gracious'.

Jaden
(alt. Jaden, Jadyn, Jaeden, Jaiden, Jaidyn, Jayden, Jaydin)
Hebrew, meaning 'Jehovah has heard'.

Jafar
Arabic, meaning 'stream'.

117

J

Jagger
Old English, meaning 'one who cuts'.

Jaheem
(alt. Jaheim)
Hebrew, meaning 'raised up'.

Jahir
Hindi, meaning 'jewel'.

Jaime
Variant for James, meaning 'he who supplants'. 'J'aime' is also French for 'I love'.

Jair
(alt. Jairo)
Hebrew, meaning 'God enlightens'.

Jake
Shortened form of Jacob, meaning 'he who supplants'.

Jalen
Greek, meaning 'healer' or 'tranquil'.

Jali
Swahili, meaning 'musician'.

Jalon
Greek, meaning 'healer' or 'tranquil'.

Jamaal
(alt. Jamal)
Arabic, meaning 'handsome'.

Jamar
(alt. Jamarcus, Jamari, Jamarion, Jamir)
Modern variant of Jamaal, meaning 'handsome'.

James
English, meaning 'he who supplants'.

Jameson
(alt. Jamison)
English, meaning 'son of James'.

Jamie
(alt. Jamey, Jaimie)
Nickname for James, meaning 'he who supplants'.

Jamil
Arabic, meaning 'handsome'.

J

Jamin

Hebrew, meaning 'son of the right hand'.

Jan
(alt. Janko, János)

Slavic, from John meaning 'the Lord is gracious'.

Janus

Latin, meaning 'gateway'. Roman god of doors, beginnings and endings.

Japhet
(alt. Japheth)

Hebrew, meaning 'comely'.

Jaquez

French form of Jacques, meaning 'God is gracious'.

Jared
(alt. Jarem, Jaren, Jaret, Jarod, Jarrod)

Hebrew, meaning 'descending'.

Jarlath

Gaelic, from Iarlaith, from Saint Iarfhlaith.

Jarom

Greek, meaning 'to raise and exalt'.

Jarrell

Variant of Gerald, meaning 'spear ruler'.

Jarrett

Old English, meaning 'spear-brave'.

Jarvis

Old German, meaning 'with honor'.

Short names

Al
Ben
Dai
Ed
Jay
Jon
Max
Rio
Sam
Ty

J

Jason
Greek, meaning 'healer'.

Jasper
Greek, meaning 'treasure holder'.

Javen
Arabic, meaning 'youth'.

Javier
Spanish, meaning 'bright'.

Jay
Latin, meaning 'jaybird'.

Jaylan
(alt. Jaylen)
Greek, meaning 'healer'.

Jeevan
Indian, meaning 'life'.

Jeffrey
(alt. Jeff)
Old German, meaning 'peace'.

Jefferson
English, meaning 'son of Jeffrey'.

Jensen
Scandinavian, meaning 'son of Jan'.

Jeremy
(alt. Jem)
Hebrew, meaning 'the Lord exalts'.

Jeriah
Hebrew, meaning 'Jehovah has seen'.

Jericho
Arabic, meaning 'city of the moon'.

Jermaine
Latin, meaning 'brotherly'.

Jerome
Greek, meaning 'sacred name'.

Jerry
English, from Gerald, meaning 'spear ruler'.

Jesse
Hebrew, meaning 'the Lord exists'.

J

Jesus

Hebrew, meaning 'the Lord is Salvation' and the Son of God.

Jethro

Hebrew, meaning 'eminent'.

Jim

(alt. Jimmy)

From James, meaning 'he who supplants'.

Jiri

(alt. Jiro)

Greek, meaning 'farmer'.

Joachim

Hebrew, meaning 'established by God'.

Joah

(alt. João)

Hebrew, meaning 'God is gracious' .

Joaquin

Hebrew, meaning 'established by God'.

Joe

(alt. Joey, Johan, Johannes, Jomar)

From Joseph, meaning 'Jehovah increases'.

Joel

Hebrew, meaning 'Jehovah is the Lord'.

John

Hebrew, meaning 'God is gracious'.

Johnny

(alt. Jon, Jonny)

From Jonathan, meaning 'gift of God'.

Jolyon

From Julian, meaning 'young'.

Jonah

(alt. Jonas)

Hebrew, meaning 'dove'.

Jonathan

(alt. Johnathan, Johnathon, Jonathon, Jonty)

Hebrew, meaning 'God is gracious'.

J

Jordan
(alt. Jory, Judd)
Hebrew, meaning 'down-flowing'.

Jorge
From George, meaning 'farmer'.

José
Spanish variant of Joseph, meaning 'God increases'.

Joseph
(alt. Joss)
Hebrew, meaning 'God increases'.

Josh
Shortened form of Joshua, meaning 'Jehovah is salvation'.

Joshua
Hebrew, meaning 'God is salvation'.

Josiah
Hebrew, meaning 'God helps'.

Josué
Spanish variant of Joshua, meaning 'God is salvation'.

Jovan
Latin, meaning 'the supreme God'.

Joyce
Latin, meaning 'joy'.

Juan
Spanish variant of John, meaning 'God is gracious'.

Jubal
Hebrew, meaning 'ram's horn'.

Jude
Hebrew, meaning 'praise' or 'thanks'.

Judson
Variant of Jude, meaning 'praise' or 'thanks'.

Jules
From Julian, meaning 'Jove's child'.

Julian
(alt. Julio)
Greek, meaning 'Jove's child'.

J

> ## 'Bad boy' names
>
> Ace
> Arnie
> Axel
> Bruce
> Buzz
> Conan
> Guy
> Rhett
> Spike
> Tyson

Julien
French variant of Julian, meaning 'Jove's child'.

Junior
Latin, meaning 'the younger one'.

Junius
Latin, meaning 'young'.

Jupiter
Latin, meaning 'the supreme God'. Jupiter was king of the Roman gods and the god of thunder.

Juraj
Hebrew, meaning 'God is my judge'.

Jurgen
Greek, meaning 'farmer'.

Justice
English, from the word 'justice'.

Justin
(alt. Justus)
Latin, meaning 'just and upright'.

Juwan
Hebrew, meaning 'the Lord is gracious'.

J

Famous male guitarists

Brian (May)
Carlos (Santana)
Chuck (Berry)
Eddie (Van Halen)
Eric (Clapton)
Frank (Zappa)
Jeff (Beck)
Jimi/Jimmy (Hendrix/Page)
Joe (Satriani)
Keith (Richards)

 **Boys' names**

Kabelo
African, meaning 'gift'.

Kade
Scottish, meaning 'from the wetlands'.

Kadeem
Arabic, meaning 'one who serves'.

Kaden
(alt. Kadin, Kaeden, Kaedin, Kaiden)
Arabic, meaning 'companion'.

Kadir
Arabic, meaning 'capable and competent'.

Kahlil
Arabic, meaning 'friend'.

Kai
Greek, meaning 'keeper of the keys'.

Kaito
Japanese, meaning 'ocean and sake dipper'.

Kalani
Hawaiian, meaning 'sky'.

Kale
German, meaning 'free man'.

Kaleb
Hebrew, meaning 'dog' or 'aggressive'.

Kalen
(alt. Kaelen, Kalan)
Gaelic, meaning 'uncertain'.

K

Kaleo
Hawaiian, meaning 'the voice'.

Kalil
Arabic, meaning 'friend'.

Kalvin
French, meaning 'bald'.

Kamari
Indian, meaning 'the enemy of desire'.

Kamden
English, meaning 'winding valley'.

Kamil
Arabic, meaning 'perfection'.

Kane
Gaelic, meaning 'little battler'.

Kani
Hawaiian, meaning 'sound'.

Kanye
African town in Botswana. Made popular by rapper Kanye West.

Kareem
(alt. Karim)
Arabic, meaning 'generous'.

Karl
(alt. Karson)
Old German, meaning 'free man'.

Kasey
(alt. Kacey)
Irish, meaning 'alert'.

Kaspar
Persian, meaning 'treasurer'.

Kavon
Gaelic, meaning 'handsome'.

Kayden
Arabic, meaning 'companion'.

Kazimierz
Polish, meaning 'declares peace'.

Kazuki
Japanese, meaning 'radiant hope'.

K

Kazuo
Japanese, meaning 'harmonious man'.

Keagan
(alt. Keegan, Kegan)
Gaelic, meaning 'small flame'.

Keane
Gaelic, meaning 'fighter'.

Keanu
Hawaiian, meaning 'breeze'.

Keary
Gaelic, meaning 'black-haired'.

Keaton
English, meaning 'place of hawks'.

Keeler
Gaelic, meaning 'beautiful and graceful'.

Keenan
(alt. Kenan)
Gaelic, meaning 'little ancient one'.

Keiji
Japanese, meaning 'govern with discretion'.

Keir
Gaelic, meaning 'dark-haired' or 'dark-skinned'.

Keith
Gaelic, meaning 'woodland'.

Kekoa
Hawaiian, meaning 'brave one' or 'soldier'.

Kelby
Old English, meaning 'farmhouse near the stream'.

Kell
(alt. Kellan, Kellen, Kelley, Kelly, Kiel)
Norse, meaning 'spring'.

Kelsey
Old English, meaning 'victorious ship'.

Kelton
Old English, meaning 'town of the keels'.

K

Kelvin
Old English, meaning 'friend of ships'.

Ken
Shortened form of Kenneth, meaning 'born of fire'.

Kendal
Old English, meaning 'the Kent river valley'.

Kendon
Old English, meaning 'brave guard'.

Kendrick
Gaelic, meaning 'royal ruler'.

Kenelm
Old English, meaning 'bold'.

Kenji
Japanese, meaning 'intelligent second son'.

Kennedy
Gaelic, meaning 'helmet head'.

Kenneth
(alt. Kenney)
Gaelic, meaning 'born of fire'.

Kennison
English, meaning 'son of Kenneth'.

Kent
From the English county.

Kenton
English, meaning 'town of Ken'.

Kenya
(alt. Kenyon)
From the country in Africa.

Kenyatta
From Kenya.

Kenzo
Japanese, meaning 'wise'.

Keola
Hawaiian, meaning 'life'.

Keon
(alt. Keoni)
Hawaiian, meaning 'gracious'.

Kepler
German, meaning 'hat maker'.

Kermit
(alt. Kerwin)

Gaelic, meaning 'without envy'. Associated with Kermit the Frog.

Kerr
English, meaning 'wetland'.

Keshav
Indian, meaning 'beautiful-haired'.

Kevin
Gaelic, meaning 'handsome beloved'.

Khalid
(alt. Khalif, Khalil)

Arabic, meaning 'immortal'.

Kian
(alt. Keyon, Kyan)

Irish, meaning 'ancient'.

Kiefer
German, meaning 'barrel maker'.

Kieran
(alt. Kieron, Kyron)

Gaelic, meaning 'black'.

Kijana
African, meaning 'youth'.

Kilby
English, from the town of the same name.

Kilian
Irish, meaning 'bright-headed'.

Kimani
African, meaning 'beautiful and sweet'.

King
English, from the word 'king'.

Kingsley
English, meaning 'the king's meadow'.

Kirby
German, meaning 'settlement by a church'.

Kirk
Old German, meaning 'church'.

Klaus
German, meaning 'victorious'.

K

129

K

Kobe
(alt. Koda, Kody)
Japanese, meaning 'a Japanese city'.

Kofi
Ghanaian, meaning 'born on Friday'.

Kohana
Japanese, meaning 'little flower'.

Kojo
Ghanaian, meaning 'Monday'.

Kolby
Norse, meaning 'settlement'.

Korbin
Gaelic, meaning 'a steep hill'.

Kramer
German, meaning 'shopkeeper'.

Kris
(alt. Krish)
From Christopher, meaning 'bearing Christ inside'.

Kurt
German, meaning 'courageous advice'.

Kurtis
French, meaning 'courtier'.

Kwame
Ghanaian, meaning 'born on Saturday'.

Kyden
English, meaning 'narrow little fire'.

Kylan
(alt. Kyle, Kyleb, Kyler)
Gaelic, meaning 'narrow and straight'.

Kyllion
Irish, meaning 'war'.

Kyree
From Cree, a Canadian tribe.

Kyros
Greek, meaning 'legitimate power'.

L Boys' names

Laban
Hebrew, meaning 'white'.

Lachlan
Gaelic, meaning 'from the land of lakes'.

Lacy
Old French, after the place in France.

Lalit
Hindi, meaning 'beautiful'.

Lamar
Old German, meaning 'water'.

Lambert
Scandinavian, meaning 'land brilliant'.

Lambros
Greek, meaning 'brilliant and radiant'.

Lamont
Old Norse, meaning 'law man'.

Lance
French, meaning 'land'.

Lancelot
Variant of Lance, meaning 'land'. The name of one of the Knights of the Round Table.

Landen
(alt. Lando, Landon, Landyn, Langdon)
English, meaning 'long hill'.

L

Lane
(alt. *Layne*)
English, from the word 'lanel'.

Lannie
(alt. *Lanny*)
German, meaning 'precious'.

Larkin
Gaelic, meaning 'rough' or 'fierce'.

Laron
French, meaning 'thief'.

Larry
Latin, from Lawrence, meaning 'man from Laurentum'.

Lars
Scandinavian variant of Lawrence, meaning 'man from Laurentum'.

Lasse
Finnish, meaning 'girl'. (Still, ironically, a boy's name.)

Laszlo
Hungarian, meaning 'glorious rule'.

Lathyn
Latin, meaning 'fighter'.

Latif
Arabic, meaning 'gentle'.

Laurel
Latin, meaning 'bay'.

Laurent
French, from Lawrence, meaning 'man from Laurentum'.

Lawrence
Latin, meaning 'man from Laurentum'.

Lawsan
Old English, meaning 'son of Lawrence'.

Lazarus
Hebrew, meaning 'God is my help'.

Leandro
Latin, meaning 'lion man'.

Lear
German, meaning 'of the meadow'.

L

Lee
(alt. Leigh)
Old English, meaning 'meadow' or 'valley'.

Leib
German, meaning 'love'.

Leif
Scandinavian, meaning 'heir'.

Leith
From the name of a place in Scotland.

Lennox
(alt. Lenny)
Gaelic, meaning 'with many Elm trees'.

Leo
Latin, meaning 'lion'.

Leon
Latin, meaning 'lion'.

Leonard
Old German, meaning 'lion strength'.

Leopold
German, meaning 'brave people'.

Leroy
French, meaning 'king'.

Lesley
(alt. Les)
Scottish, meaning 'holly garden'.

Lester
English, meaning 'from Leicester'.

Lewis
French, meaning 'renowned fighter'.

Liam
German, meaning 'helmet'.

Lincoln
English, meaning 'lake colony'.

Lindsay
Scottish, meaning 'linden tree'.

Linus
Latin, meaning 'lion'.

Lionel
English, meaning 'lion'.

L

Llewellyn
Welsh, meaning 'like a lion'.

Lloyd
Welsh, meaning 'gray-haired and sacred'.

Logan
Gaelic, meaning 'hollow'.

Lonnie
English, meaning 'lion strength'.

Lorcan
Gaelic, meaning 'little fierce one'.

Louis
(alt. Lou, Louie, Luigi, Luis)
German, meaning 'famous warrior'.

Lucian
(alt. Lucio)
Latin, meaning 'light'.

Ludwig
German, meaning 'famous fighter'.

Luke
(alt. Luc, Luka)
Latin, meaning 'from Lucanus' (in southern Italy).

Lupe
Latin, meaning 'wolf'.

Luther
German, meaning 'soldier of the people'.

Lyle
French, meaning 'the island'.

Lyn
(alt. Lyndon)
Spanish, meaning 'pretty'.

M Boys' names

Mac
(alt. Mack, Mackie)
Scottish, meaning 'son of'.

Macaulay
Scottish, meaning 'son of the phantom'.

Mace
English, meaning 'heavy staff' or 'club'.

Mackenzie
Scottish, meaning 'the fair one'.

Mackland
Scottish, meaning 'land of Mac'.

Macon
French, from the name of towns in France and Georgia.

Macsen
Scottish, meaning 'son of Mac'.

Madden
Irish, meaning 'descendant of the hound'.

Maddox
English, meaning 'good' or 'generous'.

Madison
(alt. Madsen)
Irish, meaning 'son of Madden'.

M

Mads

Shortened form of Madden, meaning 'descendant of the hound'.

Magnus
(alt. Manus)

Latin, meaning 'great'.

Maguire

Gaelic, meaning 'son of the beige one'.

Mahesh

Hindi, meaning 'great ruler'.

Mahir

Arabic, meaning 'skillful'.

Mahlon

Hebrew, meaning 'sickness'.

Mahmoud

Arabic, meaning 'praise-worthy'.

Mahoney

Irish, meaning 'bear'.

Major

English, from the word 'major'.

Makal

From Michael, meaning 'close to God'.

Makani

Hawaiian, meaning 'wind'.

Makis

Hebrew, meaning 'gift from God'.

Mako

Hebrew, meaning 'God is with us'.

Malachi
(alt. Malachy)

Irish, meaning 'messenger of God'.

Malcolm

English, meaning 'Columba's servant'.

Mali

Arabic, meaning 'full and rich'.

Manfred

Old German, meaning 'man of peace'.

M

Manish
English, meaning 'manly'.

Manley
English, meaning 'manly and brave'.

Mannix
Gaelic, meaning 'little monk'.

Manoi
(alt. Manos)
Japanese, meaning 'love springing from intellect'.

Manuel
Hebrew, meaning 'God is with us'.

Manzi
Italian, meaning 'steer'.

Marc
(alt. Marco, Marcos, Marcus, Markel)
French, meaning 'from the god Mars'.

Marcel
(alt. Marcelino, Marcello)
French, meaning 'little warrior'.

Marek
Polish variant of Mark, meaning 'from the god Mars'.

Mariano
Latin, meaning 'from the god Mars'.

Mario
(alt. Marius)
Latin, meaning 'manly'.

Mark
English, meaning 'from the god Mars'.

Marley
(alt. Marlin, Marlow)
Old English, meaning 'meadow near the lake'.

Marlon
English origin, meaning 'little hawk' made famous by actor Marlon Brando.

Marshall
Old French, meaning 'caretaker of horses'.

Martin
(alt. Marty)
Latin, meaning 'dedicated to Mars'.

Marvel
English, from the word 'marvel'.

Marvin
Welsh, meaning 'sea friend'.

Mason
English, from the word mason.

Mathias
(alt. Matthias)
Hebrew, meaning 'gift of God'.

Mathieu
French form of Matthew, meaning 'gift of the Lord'.

Matthew
Hebrew, meaning 'gift of the Lord'.

Maurice
(alt. Mauricio)
Latin, meaning 'dark skinned' or 'Moorish'.

Maverick
American, meaning 'non-conformist leader'.

Max
(alt. Maxie, Maxim)
Latin, meaning 'greatest'.

Maximillian
Latin, meaning 'greatest'.

Maximino
Latin, meaning 'little Max'.

Maxwell
Latin, meaning 'Maccus' stream'.

Maynard
Old German, meaning 'brave'.

McArthur
Scottish, meaning 'son of Arthur'.

McCoy
Scottish, meaning 'son of Coy'.

Mearl
English, meaning 'my earl'.

Mederic
French, meaning 'doctor'.

M

Mekhi

African, meaning 'who is God?'.

Mel

Gaelic, meaning 'smooth brow'.

Melbourne

From the city in Australia.

Melchior

Persian, meaning 'king of the city'.

Melton

English, meaning 'town of Mel'.

Melva

Hawaiian, meaning 'plumeria'.

Melville

Scottish, meaning 'town of Mel'.

Melvin

(alt. Melvyn)

English, meaning 'smooth brow'.

Memphis

Greek, meaning 'established and beautiful'.

Mercer

English, from the word 'mercer'.

Merl

French, meaning 'blackbird'.

Merlin

Welsh, meaning 'sea fortress'.

Merrick

Welsh, meaning 'Moorish'.

Merrill

Gaelic, meaning 'shining sea'.

Merritt

English, from the word 'merit'.

Merton

Old English, meaning 'town by the lake'.

Meyer

Hebrew, meaning 'bright farmer'.

M

Michael

Hebrew, meaning 'resembles God'.

Michalis
(alt. Miklos)

Greek form of Michael, meaning 'resembles God'.

Michel

French form of Michael, meaning 'resembles God'.

Michelangelo

Italian, meaning 'Michael's angel'. Name of the famous Italian artist.

Michele

Italian form of Michael, meaning 'resembles God'.

Miguel

Spanish form of Michael meaning 'resembles God'.

Mike
(alt. Mickey, Mikie)

Shortened form of Michael meaning 'resembles God'.

Milan

From the name of the Italian city.

Miles
(alt. Milo, Milos, Myles)

English, from the word 'miles'.

Milton

English, meaning 'miller's town'.

Miro

Slavic, meaning 'peace'.

Misha

Russian, meaning 'who is like God'.

Mitch

Shortened form of Mitchell, meaning 'who is like God'.

Mitchell

English, meaning 'who is like God'.

Modesto

Italian, meaning 'modest'.

M

Football players

Bart (Starr)
Deacon (Jones)
Dick (Butkus)
Emmitt (Smith)
Jerry (Rice)
Jim (Brown)
Joe (Namath/Montana)
John/Johnny (Elway Unitas)

Moe
Hebrew, meaning 'God's helmet'.

Mohamed
(alt. Mohammad, Mohamet, Mohammed)
Arabic, meaning 'praiseworthy'.

Monroe
Gaelic, meaning 'mouth of the river Rotha'.

Monserrate
Latin, meaning 'jagged mountain'.

Montague
French, meaning 'pointed hill'.

Montana
Latin, meaning 'mountain'.

Monte
Italian, meaning 'mountain'.

Montgomery
Variant of Montague, meaning 'pointed hill'.

Monty
Shortened form of Montague, meaning 'pointed hill'.

Moody
English, from the word 'moody'.

Mordecai
Hebrew, meaning 'little man'.

Morgan
Welsh, meaning 'circling sea'.

Moritz
Latin, meaning 'dark skinned and Moorish'.

Morpheus
Greek, meaning 'shape'.

M

Morris
Welsh, meaning 'dark-skinned and Moorish'.

Morrison
English, meaning 'son of Morris'.

Mortimer
French, meaning 'dead sea'.

Morton
Old English, meaning 'moor town'.

Moses
(alt. Moshe, Moshon)
Hebrew, meaning 'savior'.

Moss
English, from the word 'moss'.

Mungo
Gaelic, meaning 'most dear'.

Murl
French, meaning 'blackbird'.

Murphy
Irish, meaning 'sea warrior'.

Murray
Gaelic, meaning 'lord and master'.

Mustafa
Arabic, meaning 'chosen'.

Myron
Greek, meaning 'myrrh'.

N

Boys' names

Najee

Arabic, meaning 'dear companion'.

Nakia

Arabic, meaning 'pure'.

Nakul

Indian, meaning 'mongoose'.

Naphtali

Hebrew, meaning 'wrestling'.

Napoleon

Italian origin, meaning 'man from Naples'. Name of the French general who became Emperor of France.

Narciso

Latin, from the myth of Narcissus, famous for drowning after gazing at his own reflection.

Nash

English, meaning 'at the ash tree'.

Nasir

Arabic, meaning 'helper'.

Nate

Hebrew, meaning 'God has given'.

Nathan

(alt. Nathaniel)

Hebrew, meaning 'God has given'.

N

Popular song names

Alexander (*Alexander's Ragtime Band*, Irving Berlin)
Daniel (*Daniel*, Elton John)
Frankie (*Frankie*, Sister Sledge)
Jack (*Jumpin' Jack Flash*, The Rolling Stones)
James (*James Dean*, The Eagles)
Johnny (*Johnny B. Goode*, Chuck Berry)
Kenneth (*What's the Frequency, Kenneth?*, REM)
Leroy (*Bad, Bad Leroy Brown*, Jim Croce)
Mack (*Mack The Knife*, Bobby Darin)
Oliver (*Oliver's Army*, Elvis Costello)

Naveen
Indian, meaning 'new'.

Neal
Irish, meaning 'champion'.

Ned
Nickname for Edward, meaning 'wealthy guard'.

Neftali
Hebrew, meaning 'struggling'.

Nehemiah
Hebrew, meaning 'comforter'.

Neil
(alt. Niall)
Irish, meaning 'champion'.

Neilson
Irish, meaning 'son of Neil'.

Nelson
Variant of Neil, meaning 'champion'

Nemo
Latin, meaning 'nobody'.

Neo
Latin, meaning 'new'.

N

Nephi
Greek, meaning 'cloud'.

Nessim
Arabic, meaning 'breeze'.

Nestor
Greek, meaning 'traveller'.

Neville
Old French, meaning 'new village'.

Newton
English, meaning 'new town'.

Nicholas
(alt. Niklas)
Greek, meaning 'victorious'.

Nick
(alt. Nico, Niko, Nikos)
Shortened form of Nicholas, meaning 'victorious'.

Nigel
Gaelic, meaning 'champion'.

Nikhil
Hindi, meaning 'whole' or 'entire'.

Nikita
Greek, meaning 'unconquered'. Also a girls' name.

Nikolai
Russian variant of Nicholas, meaning 'victorious'.

Nimrod
Hebrew, meaning 'we will rebel'.

Nissim
Hebrew, meaning 'wonderful things'.

Noah
Hebrew, meaning 'peaceful'.

Noel
French, meaning 'Christmas'.

Nolan
Gaelic, meaning 'champion'.

Norbert
Old German, meaning 'Northern brightness'.

N

Norman

Old German, meaning 'Northerner'.

Normand

French, meaning 'from Normandy'.

Norris

Old French, meaning 'Northerner'.

Norton

English, meaning 'Northern town'.

Norval

French, meaning 'Northern town'.

Norwood

English, meaning 'Northern forest'.

Nova

Latin, meaning 'new'.

Nuno

Latin, meaning 'ninth'.

Nunzio

Italian, meaning 'messenger'.

Names of Gods

Anubis (Death: Egyptian)
Apollo (Sun: Roman)
Brahma (Creation: Indian)
Eros (Love: Greek)
Hypnos (Sleep: Greek)
Mars (War: Roman)
Neptune (Sea: Roman)
Ra (Sun: Egyptian)
Shiva (Destruction: Indian)
Vishnu (Preservation: Indian)

O Boys' names

Oakley

English, meaning 'from the oak meadow'.

Obadiah

Hebrew, meaning 'God's worker'.

Obama

African, meaning 'crooked'.

Obed

Hebrew, meaning 'servant of God'.

Spelling options

A vs E (Aiden or Aidan)
F vs PH (Josef or Joseph)
I vs Y (Henri or Henry)
J vs G (Jorge or George)
N vs HN (Jon or John)
QUE vs CK (Frederique or Frederick)

O

Oberon

Old German, meaning 'royal bear'.

Obie

Shortened form of Oberon, meaning 'royal bear'.

Octave

(alt. Octavian, Octavio)

Latin, meaning 'eight'.

Oda

(alt. Odell, Odie, Odis)

Hebrew, meaning 'praise God'.

Ogden

Old English, meaning 'oak valley'.

Oisin

From the Irish poet.

Ola

Norse, meaning 'precious'.

Olaf

(alt. Olan)

Old Norse, meaning 'ancestor'.

Oleander

Hawaiian, meaning 'joyous'.

Oleg

(alt. Olen)

Russian, meaning 'holy'.

Olin

Russian, meaning 'rock'.

Oliver

Latin, meaning 'olive tree'.

Olivier

French form of Oliver, meaning 'olive tree'.

Ollie

Shortened form of Oliver, meaning 'olive tree'.

Omar

(alt. Omari, Omarion)

Arabic, meaning 'speaker'.

Ora

Latin, meaning 'hour'.

O

Oran
(alt. Oren, Orrin)
Gaelic, meaning 'light and pale'.

Orange
English, from the word 'orange'.

Orion
From the Greek hunter.

Orlando
(alt. Orlo)
Old German, meaning 'old land'.

Orpheus
Greek, meaning 'beautiful voice'.

Orson
Latin, meaning 'bear'.

Orville
Old French, meaning 'gold town'.

Osaka
From the Japanese city.

Osborne
Norse, meaning 'bear god'.

Oscar
Old English, meaning 'spear of the Gods'.

Oswald
German, meaning 'God's power'.

Foreign alternatives
David – Dafydd, Dann
John – Jean, Juan
Joseph – Giuseppe, José
Michael – Miguel, Mikhail
Owen – Eoghan, Owain
Peter – Pedro, Pierre, Pieter
Richard – Ricardo

Otha
(alt. Otho)
German, meaning 'wealth'.

Othello
Old German, meaning 'wealth'. From the Shakespearean character.

Otis
German, meaning 'wealth'.

Otten
English, meaning 'otter-like'.

Otto
Italian, meaning 'eight'.

Owain
Welsh, meaning 'youth'.

Owen
Welsh, meaning 'well born and noble'.

Oz
Hebrew, meaning 'strength'.

Popular Asian names for boys and girls

Bao
Cái
Huang
Jiro
Kei
Ming
Miyoko
Shen
Tai
Yoko

P

Boys' names

Pablo
Spanish, meaning 'little'.

Padma
Indian, meaning 'lotus'.

Padraig
Irish, meaning 'noble'.

Panos
Greek, meaning 'all holy'.

Paolo
Italian, meaning 'little'.

Paresh
Indian, meaning 'supreme standard'.

Parker
Old English, meaning 'park keeper'.

Pascal
Latin, meaning 'Easter child'.

Pat
Shortened form of Patrick, meaning 'noble'.

Patrick
(alt. Patrice)
Irish, meaning 'noble'.

Patten
English, meaning 'noble'.

Paul
Hebrew, meaning 'small'.

P

Pavel

Latin, meaning 'small'.

Pax

Latin, meaning 'peace'.

Paxton

English, meaning 'town of peace'.

Payne

Latin, meaning 'peasant'.

Payton

Latin, meaning 'peasant's town'.

Pedro

Spanish form of Peter, meaning 'rock'.

Penn

English, meaning 'hill'.

Percival

French, meaning 'pierce the valley'.

Percy

Shortened form of Percival, meaning 'pierce the valley'.

Perez

Hebrew, meaning 'breach'.

Pericles

Greek, meaning 'far-famed'.

Perrin

Greek, meaning 'rock'.

Perry

English, meaning 'rock'.

Pervis

English, meaning 'purveyor'.

Pete

Shortened form of Peter, meaning 'rock'.

Peter

Greek, meaning 'rock'.

Petros

Greek form of Peter, meaning 'rock'.

Peyton

Old English, meaning 'fighting man's estate'.

P

Phil
Shortened form of Philip, meaning 'lover of horses'.

Philip
Greek, meaning 'lover of horses'.

Philo
Greek, meaning 'love'.

Phineas
(alt. Pinchas)
Hebrew, meaning 'oracle'.

Phoenix
Greek, meaning 'dark red'.

Pierre
French form of Peter, meaning 'rock'.

Piers
Greek form of Peter, meaning 'rock'.

Pierson
Variant of Pierce, meaning 'son of Piers'.

Pip
Greek, meaning 'lover of horses'.

Placido
Latin, meaning 'placid'.

Pradeep
Hindi, meaning 'light'.

Pranav
Hindi, meaning 'spiritual leader'.

Presley
Old English, meaning 'priest's meadow'.

Preston
Old English, meaning 'priest's town'.

No-nickname names

Alex
Jude
Keith
Otto
Owen
Toby

P

Primo
Italian, meaning 'first'.

Primus
Latin, meaning 'first'.

Prince
English, from the word 'prince'.

Prospero
Latin, meaning 'prosperous'.

Pryce
(alt. Prize)
Old French, meaning 'prize'.

Pryor
English, meaning 'first'.

Ptolemy
Greek, meaning 'aggressive' or 'warlike'.

Boys' names

Quabil

Arabic, meaning 'able'.

Quadim

Arabic, meaning 'able'.

Quadir

Arabic, meaning 'powerful'.

Quaid

Irish, meaning 'fourth'.

Quemby

Norse, meaning 'from the woman's estate'.

Quentin

(alt. Quinten, Quintin, Quinton, Quintus)

Latin, meaning 'fifth'.

Quillan

Gaelic, meaning 'sword'.

Quillon

Gaelic, meaning 'club'.

Quincy

Old French, meaning 'estate of the fifth son'.

Quinlan

Gaelic, meaning 'fit, shapely and strong'.

Quinn

Gaelic, meaning 'counsel'.

'Powerful' names

Americo	Oswald
Derek	Oz
Hercules	Roderick
Michio	Thor

R Boys' names

Radames
Slavic, meaning 'famous joy'.

Raekwon
Hebrew, meaning 'God has healed'.

Rafael
(alt. Rafe, Rafer, Raffi, Raphael)
Hebrew, meaning 'God has healed'.

Ragnar
Old Norse, meaning 'judgement warrior'.

Raheem
Arabic, meaning 'merciful and kind'.

Rahm
Hebrew, meaning 'pleasing'.

Rahul
(alt. Raoul, Raul)
Indian, meaning 'efficient'.

Raiden
(alt. Rainen)
From the Japanese god of thunder.

Rainen
Old German, meaning 'deciding warrior'.

Raj
Indian, meaning 'king'.

Rajesh
(alt. Ramesh)
Indian, meaning 'ruler of kings'.

Raleigh
Old English, meaning 'deer's meadow'.

R

Ralph

Old English, meaning 'wolf'.

Ram

English, from the word 'ram'.

Ramiro

Germanic, meaning 'powerful in battle'.

Ramsey
(alt. Ramsay)

Old English, meaning 'wild garlic island'.

Randall
(alt. Randolph)

Old German, meaning 'wolf shield'.

Randy

Variant of Randall, meaning 'wolf shield'. In modern English, randy can also mean amorous.

Raniel

English, meaning 'God is my happiness'.

Ranjit

Indian, meaning 'influenced by charm'.

Rannoch

Gaelic, meaning 'fern'.

Rashad

Arabic, meaning 'good judgment'.

Rasheed
(alt. Rashid)

Indian, meaning 'rightly guided'.

Rasmus

Greek, meaning 'beloved'.

Raven

English, from the word 'raven'.

Ravi

French, meaning 'delighted'.

Ray

English, from the word 'ray'.

Raymond
(alt. Rayner)

English, meaning 'advisor'.

Raz

Israeli, meaning 'secret' or 'mystery'.

R

Reagan
Irish, meaning 'little king'.

Reggie
Latin, meaning 'queen'.

Reginald
Latin, meaning 'regal'.

Regis
Shortened form of Reginald, meaning 'regal'.

Reid
Old English, meaning 'by the reeds'.

Reilly
English, meaning 'courageous'.

Remus
Latin, meaning 'swift'.

Rémy
French, meaning 'from Rheims'.

Ren
Shortened form of Reginald, meaning 'regal'.

Renato
Latin, meaning 'rebirth'.

Rene
French, meaning 'rebirth'.

Reno
Latin, meaning 'renewed'.

Reuben
Spanish, meaning 'a son'.

Reuel
Hebrew, meaning 'friend of God'.

Rex
Latin, meaning 'king'.

Rey
Spanish, meaning 'king'.

Reynold
Latin, meaning 'king's advisor'.

Rhodes
German, meaning 'where the roses grow'. Also the name of the Greek town.

Rhodri
Welsh, meaning 'ruler of the circle'.

R

Rhys
(alt. Reece, Riece)
Welsh, meaning 'enthusiasm'.

Richard
(alt. Ricardo, Rikardo)
Old German, meaning 'powerful leader'.

Richie
Shortened form of Richard, meaning 'powerful leader'.

Ricki
(alt. Ricki)
Shortened form of Richard, meaning 'powerful leader'.

Ricky
(alt. Ricki)
Shortened form of Richard, meaning 'powerful leader'.

Ridley
English, meaning 'cleared wood'.

Rigby
English, from the place in Lancashire.

Riky
Irish Gaelic, meaning 'courageous'.

Ringo
English, meaning 'ring'.

Rio
Spanish, meaning 'river'.

Riordan
Gaelic, meaning 'bard'.

Rishi
Variant of Richard, meaning 'powerful leader'.

Ritchie
Shortened form of Richard, meaning 'powerful leader'.

Roald
Scandinavian, meaning 'ruler'.

Rob
(alt. Robbie)
Shortened form of Robert, meaning 'bright fame'.

Robert
Old German, meaning 'bright fame'.

Roberto
Variant of Robert, meaning 'bright fame'.

R

Robin
English, from the word 'robin'.

Robinson
English, meaning 'son of Robin'.

Rocco
(alt. Rocky)
Italian, meaning 'rest'.

Rod
Short for both Rhodri and Rodney.

Roderick
German, meaning 'famous power'.

Rodney
Old German, meaning 'island near the clearing'.

Rodrigo
Spanish form of Roderick, meaning 'famous power'.

Roger
Old German, meaning 'spear man'.

Roland
Old German, meaning 'renowned land'.

Rolf
Old German, meaning 'wolf'.

Rollie
(alt. Rollo)
Old German, meaning 'renowned land'.

Roman
Latin, meaning 'from Rome'.

Romeo
Latin, meaning 'pilgrim to Rome'. Made famous by Shakespeare's play.

Ron
(alt. Ronnie)
Shortened form of Ronald, meaning 'mountain of strength'.

Ronald
Norse, meaning 'mountain of strength'.

Ronan
Gaelic, meaning 'little seal'.

R

Rory
English, meaning 'red king'.

Ross
(alt. Russ)
Scottish, meaning 'cape'.

Rowan
(alt. Roan)
Gaelic, meaning 'little red one'.
Also reference to the rowan
tree.

Roy
Gaelic, meaning 'red'.

Ruben
Hebrew, meaning 'son'.

Rudolph
Old German, meaning 'famous
wolf'.

Rudy
Shortened form of Rudolph,
meaning 'famous wolf'.

Rufus
Latin, meaning 'red-haired'.

Rupert
Variant of Robert, meaning
'bright fame'.

Russell
Old French, meaning 'little
red one'.

Rusty
English, meaning 'ruddy'.

Ryan
Gaelic, meaning 'little king'.

Ryder
English, meaning 'horseman'.

Rye
English, from the word 'rye'.

Ryker
From Richard, meaning
'powerful leader'.

Rylan
English, meaning 'land where
rye is grown'.

Ryley
Old English, meaning 'rye
clearing'.

S

Boys' names

Saber
French, meaning 'sword'.

Sagar
African, meaning 'ruler of the water'.

Sage
English, meaning 'wise'.

Sakari
Native American, meaning 'sweet'.

Salim
Arabic, meaning 'secure'.

Salvador
Spanish, meaning 'savior'.

Salvatore
Italian, meaning 'savior'.

Sam
(alt. Sama, Sammie, Sammy)
Hebrew, meaning 'God is heard'. Shortened form of Samuel.

Samir
Arabic, meaning 'pleasant companion'.

Spring names

Alvern
Jarek
Kell
Marcus
Tamiko

S

Samson
Hebrew, meaning 'son of Sam'.

Samuel
Hebrew, meaning 'God is heard'.

Sandeep
Indian, meaning 'lighting the way'.

Sandro
Shortened form of Alessandro, meaning 'defending men'.

Sandy
Shortened form of Alexander, Greek meaning 'defending men'.

Sanjay
Indian, meaning 'victory'.

Santana
Spanish, meaning 'saint'.

Santiago
Spanish, meaning 'Saint James'.

Santino
Spanish, meaning 'little Saint James'.

Santo
(alt. Santos)
Latin, meaning 'saint'.

Sascha
(alt. Sacha, Sasha)
Shortened Russian form of Alexander, meaning 'defending men'.

Sawyer
English, meaning 'one who saws wood'.

Scott
(alt. Scottie)
English, meaning 'from Scotland'.

Seamus
Irish variant of James, meaning 'he who supplants'.

Sean
(alt. Shaun)
Variant of John, meaning 'God is gracious'.

Sebastian
Greek, meaning 'revered'.

Sébastien
French form of Sebastian, meaning 'revered'.

S

Sergio

Latin, meaning 'servant'.

Seth

Hebrew, meaning 'appointed'.

Severus

Latin, meaning 'severe'.

Seymour

English, from the place name in northern France.

Shane

Variant of Sean, meaning 'God is gracious'.

Sharif

Arabic, meaning 'honored'.

Shea

Gaelic, meaning 'admirable'.

Shelby

Norse, meaning 'willow'.

Sherlock

English, meaning 'fair-haired'.

Sherman

Old English, meaning 'shear man'.

Shmuel

Hebrew, meaning 'his name is God'.

Shola

Arabic, meaning 'energetic'.

Sid

Shortened form of Sidney, meaning 'wide meadow'.

Sidney

English, meaning 'wide meadow'.

Sigmund

Old German, meaning 'victorious hand'.

Silvanus

(alt. Silvio)

Latin, meaning 'woods'.

Summer names

Augustus
Balder
Leo
Sky
Somers

S

Sim

Arabic, shortened form of Simba, meaning 'lion'.

Simba

Arabic, meaning 'lion'.

Simon

(alt. Simeon)

Hebrew, meaning 'to hear'.

Sinbad

Literary merchant adventurer.

Sindri

Norse, meaning 'dwarf'.

Sipho

African, meaning 'the unknown one'.

Sire

English, from the word 'sire'.

Sirius

Hebrew, meaning 'brightest star'.

Skipper

English, meaning 'ship captain'.

Skyler

Dutch, meaning 'guarded' or 'scholar'.

Solomon

Hebrew, meaning 'peace'.

Sonny

American English, meaning 'son'.

Soren

Scandinavian, meaning 'brightest star'.

Spencer

English, meaning 'dispenser'.

Spike

English, from the word 'spike'.

Stan

Shortened form of Stanley, meaning 'stony meadow'.

Stanford

English, meaning 'stone ford'.

Stanley

English, meaning 'stony meadow'.

S

Stavros
Greek, meaning 'crowned'.

Stellan
Latin, meaning 'starred'.

Steno
German, meaning 'stone'.

Stephen
(alt. Stefan, Stefano, Steffan)
English, meaning 'crowned'.

Steven
(alt. Steve, Stevie)
English, meaning 'crowned'.

Stewart
English, meaning 'steward'.

Stoney
English, meaning 'stone like'.

Storm
English, from the word 'storm'.

Stuart
English, meaning 'steward'.

Sven
Norse, meaning 'boy'.

Sydney
English, meaning 'wide meadow'. Also a city in Australia.

Syed
Arabic, meaning 'lucky'.

Sylvester
Latin, meaning 'wooded'.

Autumn names

Aki
Akiko
Demitrius
George
Goren

S

Popular Australian names for boys and girls

Adelaide	Hobart
Brad	Lorrae
Darwin	Narelle
Evonne	Raelene
Griffith	Tallara

T Boys' names

Tacitus

Latin, meaning 'silent, calm' from the Roman historian.

Tad

English, from the word 'tadpole'.

Taj

Indian, meaning 'crown'.

Takashi

Japanese, meaning 'praiseworthy'.

Takoda

Sioux, meaning 'friend to everyone'.

Talbot

(alt. Tal)

Aristocratic English name.

Tamir

Arabic, meaning 'tall and wealthy'.

Tanner

Old English, meaning 'leather-maker'.

Taras

(alt. Tarez)

Scottish, meaning 'crag'.

Tarek

Arabic, meaning 'evening caller'.

Tarian

Welsh, meaning 'silver'.

Tariq

Arabic, meaning 'morning star'.

169

T

Tarquin

Latin, from the Roman clan name.

Tarun

Hindi, meaning 'young'.

Tatanka

Hebrew, meaning 'bull'.

Tate

English, meaning 'cheerful'.

Taurean

English, meaning 'bull-like'.

Tavares

English, meaning 'descendant of the hermit'.

Tave

(alt. Tavian, Tavis, Tavish)

French, from Gustave, meaning 'royal staff'.

Taylor

English, meaning 'tailor'.

Ted

(alt. Teddy)

English, from Edward, meaning 'wealthy guard'.

Terence

(alt. Terrill, Terry)

English, meaning 'tender'.

Tex

English, meaning 'Texan'.

Thane

(alt. Thayer)

Scottish, meaning 'landholder'.

Thatcher

(alt. Thaxter)

Old English, meaning 'roof thatcher'.

Thelonius

Latin, meaning 'ruler of the people'.

Theo

Shortened form of Theodore, meaning 'God's gift'.

Theodore

Greek, meaning 'God's gift'.

Theophile

Latin, meaning 'God's love'.

Theron

Greek, meaning 'hunter'.

Thierry

French variant of Terence, meaning 'tender'.

Thomas

Aramaic, meaning 'twin'.

Thomsen

(alt. Thomson)

English, meaning 'son of Thomas'.

Thor

Norse, meaning 'thunder'.

Tiago

From Santiago, meaning 'Saint James'.

Tiberius

English, meaning 'from the river Tiber'.

Tibor

Latin, from the river Tiber.

Tiernan

Gaelic, meaning 'lord'.

Tilden

(alt. Till)

English, meaning 'fertile valley'.

Tim

(alt. Timmie, Timon)

Shortened form of Timothy, meaning 'God's honor'.

Timothy

Greek, meaning 'God's honor'.

Tito

(alt. Titus, Tizian)

Latin, meaning 'defender'.

Tobias

(alt. Toby)

Hebrew, meaning 'God is good'.

Tod

(alt. Todd)

English, meaning 'fox'.

Tom

(alt. Tomlin, Tommy)

Aramaic, meaning 'twin'.

Tonneau

French, meaning 'barrel'.

Tony

Shortened form of Anthony, from the old Roman family name.

T

T

Torey
Norse, meaning 'Thor'.

Torin
Gaelic, meaning 'chief'.

Torquil
Gaelic, meaning 'helmet'.

Toshi
Japanese, meaning 'reflection'.

Travis
French, meaning 'crossover'.

Trevor
(alt. Tvevin)
Welsh origin, meaning 'great settlement'.

Trey
(alt. Tyree)
French, meaning 'very'.

Tristan
(alt. Tristram)
Celtic from the Celtic hero.

Troy
Gaelic, meaning 'descended from the soldier'.

Tudor
Variant of Theodore, 'God's gift'.

Tyler
English, meaning 'tile maker'.

Tyrell
French, meaning 'puller'.

Tyrone
Gaelic, meaning 'Owen's county'.

Tyson
English, meaning 'son of Tyrone'.

Winter names

Aquilo
Caldwell
Jack
Mistral
Rain

U

Boys' names

Uberto
(alt. Umberto)
Italian, variant of Hubert, meaning 'bright or shining intellect'.

Udo
German, meaning 'power of the wolf'.

Ugo
Italian form of Hugo, meaning 'mind and heart'.

Ulf
German, meaning 'wolf'.

Ulrich
German, meaning 'noble ruler'.

Ultan
Irish, meaning 'from Ulster'.

Ulysses
Greek, meaning 'wrathful'. Made famous by the mythological voyager.

Upton
English, meaning 'high town'.

Urho
Finnish, meaning 'brave'.

Uri
(alt. Uriah, Urias)
Hebrew, meaning 'my light'.

Uriel
Hebrew, meaning 'angel of light'.

U

Usher

English, from the word 'usher'.
Made famous by the R&B star.

Uzi

Hebrew, meaning 'my strength'.

Uzzi

(alt. Uzziah)

Hebrew, meaning 'my power'.

Christmas names

Casper
Celyn
Christian
Gabriel
Jesus
Joseph
Nicholas
Noel

V

V

Boys' names

Vadim
Russian, meaning 'scandal maker'.

Valdemar
German, meaning 'renowned leader'.

Valente
Latin, meaning 'valiant'.

Valentine
(alt. Val, Valentin)
English, from the word 'valentine'.

Valentino
Italian, meaning 'valentine'.

Valerio
Italian, meaning 'valiant'.

Van
Dutch, meaning 'son of'.

Vance
English, meaning 'marshland'.

Vangelis
Greek, meaning 'good news'.

Varun
Hindi, meaning 'water god'.

Vasilis
Greek, meaning 'kingly'.

Vaughan
Welsh, meaning 'little'.

Vernell
French, meaning 'green and flourishing'.

V

Verner
German, meaning 'army defender'.

Vernon
(alt. Vernie)
French, meaning 'alder grove'.

Versilius
Latin, meaning 'flier'.

Vester
Latin, meaning 'wooded'.

Victor
Latin, meaning 'champion'.

Vidal
(alt. Vidar)
Spanish, meaning 'life-giving'.

Vijay
Hindi, meaning 'conquering'.

Vikram
Hindi, meaning 'sun'.

Viktor
Latin, meaning 'victory'.

Ville
French, meaning 'town'.

Vincent
(alt. Vince)
English, meaning 'victorious'.

Virgil
Latin, meaning 'staff bearer'. From the Latin poet.

Vito
Spanish, meaning 'life'.

Vittorio
Italian, meaning 'victory'.

Vitus
Latin, meaning 'life'.

Vivian
Latin, meaning 'lively'.

Vladimir
Slavic, meaning 'prince'.

Volker
German, meaning 'defender of the people'.

Von
Norse, meaning 'hope'.

Boys' names

Wade

English, meaning 'to move forward' or 'to go'.

Waldemar

German, meaning 'famous ruler'.

Walden

English, meaning 'valley of the Britons'.

Waldo

Old German, meaning 'rule'.

Walker

English, meaning 'a fuller'.

Wallace

English, meaning 'foreigner' or 'stranger'.

Wally

German, meaning 'ruler of the army'.

Walter

(alt. Walt)

German, meaning 'ruler of the army'.

Ward

English, meaning 'guardian'.

Wardell

Old English, meaning 'watchman's hill'.

Warner

German, meaning 'army guard'.

Warren
German, meaning 'guard' or 'the game park'.

Washington
English, meaning 'clever' or 'clever man's settlement'.

Wassily
Greek, meaning 'royal' or 'kingly'.

Watson
English, meaning 'son' or 'son of Walter'.

Waverley
(alt. Waverly)
English, meaning 'quaking aspen'.

Waylon
English, meaning 'land by the road'.

Wayne
English, meaning 'a cartwright'.

Webster
English, meaning 'weaver'.

Weldon
English, meaning 'from the hill of well' or 'hill with a well'.

Wendell
(alt. Wendel)
German, meaning 'a wend'.

Werner
German, meaning 'army guard'.

Weston
English, meaning 'from the west town'.

Wheeler
English, meaning 'wheel maker'.

Whitley
English, meaning 'white wood'.

Whitman
Old English, meaning 'white man'.

Whitney
Old English, meaning 'white island'.

W

Wilber
(alt. Wilbur)

Old German, meaning 'bright will'.

Wiley

Old English, meaning 'beguiling' or 'enchanting'.

Wilford

Old English, meaning 'the ford by the willows'.

Wilfredo
(alt. Wilfred, Wilfrid)

English, meaning 'to will peace'.

Wilhelm

German, meaning 'strong-willed warrior'.

Wilkes
(alt. Wilkie)

Old English, meaning 'strong-willed protector' or 'strong and resolute protector'.

William
(alt. Will, Willie)

English (Teutonic), meaning 'strong protector' or 'strong-willed warrior'.

Willis

English, meaning 'server of William'.

Willoughby

Old Norse and Old English, meaning 'from the farm by the trees'.

Wilmer

English (Teutonic), meaning 'famously resolute'.

Wilmot

English, meaning 'resolute mind'.

Wilson

English, meaning 'son of William'.

Wilton

Old Norse and English, meaning 'from the farm by the brook/streams'.

Windell
(alt. Wendell)

German, meaning 'wanderer' or 'seeker'.

Windsor

Old English, meaning 'river bank' or 'landing place'.

Winfield

English, meaning 'from the field of Wina'.

Winslow

Old English, meaning 'victory on the hill'.

Winter

Old English, meaning 'to be born in the winter'.

Winthrop

Old English, meaning 'village of friends'.

Winton

Old English, meaning 'a friend's farm'.

Wirrin

Aboriginal, meaning 'a tea tree'.

Wistan

Old English, meaning 'battle stone' or 'mark of the battle'.

Food-inspired names

Ale
Basil
Berry
Cane
Chuck
Graham
Herb
Kale
Reuben
Rye
Shad
Tamir

Wittan

Old English, meaning 'farm in the woods' or 'farm by the woods'.

Wolf

(alt. Wolfe)

English, meaning 'strong as a wolf'.

Wolfgang

Teutonic, meaning 'the path of wolves'.

Wolfrom

Teutonic, meaning 'raven wolf'.

Wolter

Dutch, a form of Walter meaning 'ruler of the army'.

Woodburn

Old English, meaning 'a stream in the woods'.

Woodrow

English, meaning 'from the row of houses by the wood'.

Woodward

English, meaning 'guardian of the forest'.

Woody

American, meaning 'path in the woods'.

Worcester

Old English, meaning 'from a Roman site'.

Worth

American, meaning 'worth much' or 'wealthy place' or 'wealth and riches'.

Wren

Old English, meaning 'tiny bird'.

Wright

Old English, meaning 'to be a craftsman' or 'from a carpenter'.

Wyatt

Teutonic, meaning 'from wood' or 'from the wide water'.

Wynn

(alt. Wyn)

Welsh, meaning 'very blessed' or 'the fair blessed one'.

Popular English names for boys and girls

Ada	Julian
Darren	Lana
Dudley	Lauren
Faith	Posy
Garrett	Rodney

 **Boys' names**

Xadrian

American, a combination of X and Adrian, meaning 'from Hadria'.

Xander

Greek, meaning 'defender of the people'.

Xanthus

Greek, meaning 'golden-haired'.

Xavier

Latin, meaning 'to the new house'.

Xenon

Greek, meaning 'the guest'.

Xerxes

Persian, meaning 'ruler of the people' or 'respected king'.

Xylander

Greek, meaning 'man of the forest'.

Bird names

Drake
Efron
Gannet
Jay
Robin

X

Popular names of US Presidents

Abraham (Lincoln)
Andrew (Jackson, Johnson)
Barack (Obama)
Franklin (Pierce, Roosevelt)
George (Washington, H. Bush, W. Bush)
James (Madison, Monroe, Knox Polk, Buchanan, Garfield, Carter)
John (Adams, Quincy Adams, Tyler, Kennedy)
Richard (Nixon)
Ronald (Reagan)
William (Henry Harrison, McKinley, Howard Taft, Clinton)

Y Boys' names

Yaal
Hebrew, meaning 'ascending' or 'one to ascend'.

Yadid
Hebrew, meaning 'the beloved one'.

Yadon
Hebrew, meaning 'against judgment'.

Yahir
Spanish, meaning 'handsome one'.

Yair
Hebrew, meaning 'the enlightening one' or 'illuminating'.

Yakiya
Hebrew, meaning 'pure' or 'bright'.

Yanis
(alt. Yannis)
Greek, a form of John meaning 'gift of God'.

Yarden
Hebrew, meaning 'to flow downward'.

Ye
Chinese, meaning 'bright one' or 'light'.

Yehuda
Hebrew, meaning 'to praise and exalt'.

Yered

Hebrew, a form of Jared, meaning 'descending'.

Yerik

Russian, meaning 'God-appointed one'.

Yervant

Armenian, meaning 'king of people'.

Yitzak

(alt. Yitzaak)

Hebrew, meaning 'laughter' or 'one who laughs'.

Ynyr

Welsh, meaning 'to honor'.

Yobachi

African, meaning 'one who prays to God' or 'prayed to God'.

Yogi

Japanese, meaning 'one who practises yoga' or 'from yoga'.

Yona

Native American, meaning 'bear'; Hebrew, meaning 'dove'.

York

Celtic, meaning 'yew tree' or 'from the farm of the yew tree'.

Yosef

Hebrew, meaning 'added by God' or 'God shall add'.

Yuri

Aboriginal, meaning 'to hear'; Japanese, meaning 'one to listen'; Russian, a form of George meaning 'farmer'.

Yves

French, meaning 'miniature archer' or 'small archer'.

Z Boys' names

Zachariah
(alt. Zac, Zach, Zachary)
Hebrew, meaning 'remembered by the Lord' or 'God has remembered'.

Zad
Persian, meaning 'my son'.

Zadok
Hebrew, meaning 'righteous one'.

Zador
Hungarian, meaning 'violent demeanor'.

Zafar
Arabic, meaning 'triumphant'.

Zaid
African, meaning 'increase the growth' or 'growth'.

Zaide
Yiddish, meaning 'the elder ones'.

Zain
(alt. Zane)
Arabic, meaning 'the handsome son'.

Zaire
African, meaning 'river from Zaire'.

Zander
Greek, meaning 'defender of my people'.

Z

Zarek

Persian, meaning 'God protect our King'.

Names from nature

Ash
Condor
Flint
River
Tiger

part three

Girls' Names

A Girls' names

A'mari

Variation of the Swahili or Muslim name Amira, meaning 'princess'.

Aanya

Variation of the Russian name Anya, meaning 'favor' or 'grace'. Also of Sanskrit origin, meaning 'the inexhaustible'.

Aaryanna

Derivative of the Latin and Greek name Ariadne meaning 'the very holy one'.

Abby
(alt. Abbey, Abbie)
Form of Abigail, meaning 'my father's joy' in Hebrew.

Abigail
(alt. Abagail, Abbigail, Abigale, Abigayle)
Hebrew, meaning 'my father's joy'.

Abilene
(alt. Abilee)
Variation of Abelena. Latin and Spanish for 'hazelnut'.

Abra

Female variation of Abraham. Also Sanskrit, meaning 'clouds'.

Abril

Spanish for the month of April. Also Latin, meaning 'open'.

Acacia

Greek, meaning 'point' or 'thorn'. Also a species of flowering trees and shrubs.

Acadia

Variation of the Greek word arcadia meaning 'paradise'. Originally, a French colony in Canada.

Ada

(alt. Adair)

Hebrew, meaning 'adornment'.

Adalee

German, meaning 'noble'.

Adalia

Hebrew, meaning 'God is my refuge'.

Addie

(alt. Addy, Adi)

Shortened form of Addison, Adelaide, Adele and Adeline.

Addison

(alt. Addisyn, Addyson)

English, meaning 'son of Adam'.

Adelaide

(alt. Adelaida)

German, popular after the rule of William IV and Queen Adelaide of England in the 19th century.

Movie inspirations

Anita (*West Side Story*)
Bonnie (*Bonnie & Clyde*)
Dorothy (*The Wizard of Oz*)
Holly (*Breakfast at Tiffany's*)
Judy (*Private Benjamin*)
Leia (*Star Wars*)
Mary (*Mary Poppins*)
Oda Mae (*Ghost*)
Ripley (*Alien*)
Sandy (*Grease*)

Adele
(alt. Adela, Adelia, Adell, Adella, Adelle)
German, meaning 'noble' or 'nobility'.

Adeline
(alt. Adalyn, Adalynn, Adelina, Adelyn)
Variant of Adelaide, meaning 'noble'.

Aden
(alt. Addien)
Hebrew, meaning 'decoration'.

Aderyn
Welsh, meaning 'bird'.

Adesina
Nigerian, meaning 'she paves the way'. Usually given to a firstborn daughter.

Adia
Variant of Ada, meaning 'decoration'.

Adina
(alt. Adena)
Hebrew, meaning 'high hopes' or 'precious'.

Adira
Hebrew, meaning 'noble' or 'powerful'. Also the north Italian city.

Adrian
Italian, from the northern city of Adria.

Adrianna
(alt. Adriana)
Variant of Adrienne, meaning 'rich' or 'dark'.

Adrienne
(alt. Adriane, Adrianne)
Greek, meaning 'rich', or Latin meaning 'dark'.

Aegle
Greek, meaning 'brightness' or 'splendor'.

Aerin
Variant of Erin, meaning 'peace-making'.

Aerith
American, with no definitive meaning.

Aero
(alt. Aeron)
Greak, meaning 'water'.

Aerolynn
Combination of the Greek Aero, meaning 'water', and the English Lynn, meaning 'waterfall'.

Africa
Celtic, meaning 'pleasant', as well as the name of the continent.

Afsaneh
Iranian, meaning 'a fairy tale'.

Afsha
Persian, meaning 'one who sprinkles light'.

Afton
Originally a place name in Scotland.

Agatha
From Saint Agatha, the patron saint of bells, meaning 'good'.

Aglaia
One of the three Greek Graces, meaning 'brilliance'.

Agnes
Greek, meaning 'virginal' or 'pure'.

Agrippina
Latin, from the expression, meaning 'born feet first'.

Aida
Arabic, meaning 'reward' or 'present'.

Aidanne
(alt. Aidan, Aidenn)
Gaelic, meaning 'fire'.

Ailbhe
Irish, meaning 'noble' or 'bright'.

Aileen
(alt. Aelinn, Aleen, Aline, Alline, Eileen)
Gaelic variant of Helen, meaning 'light'.

Ailith
(alt. Ailish)
Old English, meaning 'seasoned warrior'.

Ailsa
Scottish, meaning 'pledge from God', as well as the name of a Scottish island.

Aimee
(alt. Aimie, Amie)
French form of Amy, meaning 'beloved'.

Aina
Scandinavian, meaning 'forever'.

Aine
(alt. Aino)
Celtic, meaning 'happiness'.

Ainsley
Scottish/Gaelic, meaning 'one's own meadow'.

Aisha
(alt. Aeysha)
Arabic, meaning 'woman'; Swahili, meaning 'life'.

Aishwarya
Variant on Aisha. Arabic, meaning 'woman'.

Aislinn
(alt. Aislin, Aisling, Aislyn, Alene, Allene)
Irish Gaelic, meaning 'dream'.

Aiyanna
(alt. Aiyana)
Native American, meaning 'forever flowering'.

Aja
Hindi, meaning 'goat'.

Akela
(alt. Akilah)
Hawaiian, meaning 'noble'.

Akilina
Greek or Russian, meaning 'eagle'.

Akiva
Hebrew, meaning 'protect and shelter'.

Alaina
(alt. Alane, Alani, Alayna, Aleena)
Feminine of Alan, originating from the Greek for 'rock' or 'comely'.

Alana
(alt. Alanna, Alannah)
Variant of Alaina, meaning 'rock' or 'comely'.

Alanis
(alt. Alarice)
Variant of Alaina, meaning 'rock' or 'comely'.

Alba

Latin for 'white'.

Alberta

(alt. Albertha, Albertine)

Feminine of Albert, from the Old German for 'noble, bright, famous'.

Albina

Latin, meaning 'white' or 'fair'.

Alda

German, meaning 'old' or 'prosperous'.

Aldis

English, meaning 'battle-seasoned'.

Aleta

(alt. Aletha)

Greek, meaning 'footloose'.

Alethea

(alt. Aletheia)

Greek, meaning 'truth'.

Alex

(alt. Alexa, Alexi, Alexia, Alexina)

Shortened version of Alexandra, meaning 'man's defender'.

Alexandra

(alt. Alejandra, Alejandrina, Alejhandra, Aleksandra, Alessandra, Alexandrea, Alexandria, Aliandra)

Feminine of Alexander, from the Greek interpretation of 'man's defender'.

Alexis

(alt. Alexus, Alexys)

Greek, meaning 'helper'.

Aleydis

Variant of Alice, meaning 'nobility'.

Alfreda

Old English, meaning 'elf power'.

Ali

(alt. Allie, Ally)

Shortened version of Alexandra, Aliyah or Alice.

Alibeth

Variant of Elizabeth, meaning 'pledged to God'.

Alice

(alt. Alize, Alyce, Alys, Alyse)

English, meaning 'noble' or 'nobility'.

Alicia

(alt. Ahlicia, Alecia, Alesia, Alessia, Alizia, Alycia, Alysia)

Variant of Alice, meaning 'nobility'.

Alida

(alt. Aleida)

Latin, meaning 'small-winged one'.

Alienor

(alt. Aliana)

Variant spelling of Eleanor. Greek, meaning 'light'.

Aliki

(alt. Alika)

Variant of Alice, meaning 'nobility'.

Alima

Arabic, meaning 'cultured'.

Alina

(alt. Alena)

Slavic, variation of Helen, meaning 'light'.

Alisha

(alt. Alesha, Alysha)

Variant of Alice, meaning 'nobility'.

Alison

(alt. Allison, Allisyn, Allyson, Alyson)

Variant of Alice, meaning 'nobility'.

Alivia

Variant of Olivia, meaning 'olive tree'.

Aliya

(alt. Aaliyah, Aleah, Alia, Aliah, Aliyah)

Arabic, meaning 'exalted' or 'sublime'.

Alla

Variant of Ella or Alexandra. Also a possible reference to Allah.

Allegra

Italian, meaning 'joyous'.

Allura

French, from the word for entice, meaning 'the power of attraction'.

Allyn

Feminine of Alan, meaning 'peaceful'.

197

Alma

Three possible origins: Latin for 'giving nurture', Italian for 'soul' and Arabic for 'learned'.

Almeda
(alt. Almeta)

Latin, meaning 'ambitious'.

Almera
(alt. Almira)

Feminine of Elmer, from the Arabic for 'aristocratic' and the Old English meaning 'noble'.

Alohi

Variant of the Hawaiian greeting Aloha, meaning 'love and affection'.

Alona

Hebrew, meaning 'oak tree'.

Alora

Variant of Alona, meaning 'oak tree'.

Alpha

The first letter of the Greek alphabet, usually given to a firstborn daughter.

Alta

Latin, meaning 'elevated'.

Altagracia

Spanish, meaning 'grace'.

Althea
(alt. Altea, Altha)

Greek, meaning 'healing power'.

Alva

Spanish, meaning 'blonde' or 'fair-skinned'.

Alvena
(alt. Alvina)

English, meaning 'noble friend'.

Alvia
(alt. Alyvia)

Variant of Olivia or Elvira.

Alyssa
(alt. Alisa, Alissa, Allyssa, Alysa)

Greek, meaning 'rational'.

Amabel

Variant of Annabel, meaning 'grace and beauty'.

Amadea

Feminine of Amadeus, meaning 'God's' love.

A

Amalia

Variant of Emilia, Latin, meaning 'rival, eager'.

Amana

Hebrew, meaning 'loyal and true'.

Amanda

Latin, meaning 'much loved'.

Amandine

Variant of Amanda, meaning 'much loved'.

Amara

(alt. Amani)

Greek, meaning 'lovely forever'.

Amarantha

Contraction of Amanda and Samantha, meaning 'much loved listener'.

Amaris

(alt. Amari, Amasa, Amata, Amaya)

Hebrew, meaning 'pledged by God'.

Amaryllis

Greek, meaning 'fresh'. Also a flower by the same name.

Amber

French, from the semi-precious stone of the same name.

Amberly

Contraction of Amber and Leigh, meaning 'stone' and 'meadow'.

Amberlynn

Contraction of Amber and Lynn, meaning 'stone' and 'waterfall'.

Amelia

(alt. Aemilia)

Greek, meaning 'industrious'.

Amelie

(alt. Amalie)

French version of Amelia, meaning 'industrious'.

America

From the country of the same name.

Ameris

Variant of amaryllis, meaning 'fresh'.

Amethyst

Greek, from the precious, mulberry colored stone of the same name.

Amina

Arabic, meaning 'honest and trustworthy'.

Amira

(alt. Amiya, Amiyah)

Arabic, meaning 'a high-born girl'.

Amity

Latin, meaning 'friendship and harmony'.

Amory

Variant of the Spanish name Amor, meaning 'love'.

Amy

(alt. Amee, Ami, Amie, Ammie)

Latin, meaning 'beloved'.

Amya

Variant of Amy, meaning 'beloved'.

Ana-Lisa

Contraction of Anna and Lisa, meaning 'grace' or 'consecrated to God'.

Anafa

Hebrew, meaning 'heron'.

Ananda

Hindi, meaning 'bliss'.

Anastasia

(alt. Athanasia)

Greek, meaning 'resurrection'.

Anatolia

From the eastern Greek town of the same name.

Andrea

(alt. Andreia, Andria)

Feminine of Andrew, from the Greek term for 'a man's woman'.

Andrine

Variant of Andrea, meaning 'a man's woman'.

Andromeda

From the heroine of a Greek legend.

Anemone

Greek, meaning 'breath'.

A

Angela
(alt. Angel, Angeles, Angelia Angelle, Angie)
Greek, meaning 'messenger from God' or 'angel'.

Angelica
(alt. Angelina, Angeline, Angelique, Angelise, Angelita, Anjelica)
Latin, meaning 'angelic'.

Anise
(alt. Anisa, Anissa)
French, from the licorice flavored plant of the same name.

Aniston
English, meaning 'town of Agnes'.

Anita
(alt. Anitra)
Variant of Ann, meaning 'grace'.

Ann
(alt. Anne, Annie)
Derived from Hannah, meaning 'grace'.

Anna
(alt. Ana, Anne)
Derived from Hannah, meaning 'grace'.

Annabel
(alt. Anabel, Anabelle, Annabell, Annabella, Annabelle)
Contraction of Anna and Belle, meaning 'grace' and 'beauty'.

Annalise
(alt. Annalee, Annalisa, Anneli, Annelie, Annelise)
Contraction of Anna and Lise, meaning 'grace' and 'pledged to God'.

Annemarie
(alt. Annamae, Annamarie, Annelle, Annmarie)
Contraction of Anna and Mary, meaning 'grace' and 'star of the sea'.

Annette
(alt. Annetta)
Derived from Hannah, Hebrew, meaning 'grace'.

Annis
Greek, meaning 'finished or completed'.

Annora
Latin, meaning 'honor'.

A

Anoushka
(alt. Anousha)

Russian variation of Ann, meaning 'grace'.

Ansley
English, meaning 'the awesome one's meadow'.

Anthea
(alt. Anthi)

Greek, meaning 'flower-like'.

Antigone
In Greek mythology, Antigone was the daughter of Oedipus.

Antoinette
(alt. Anonetta, Antonette, Antonietta)

Both a variation of Ann and the feminine of Anthony, meaning 'invaluable grace'.

Antonia
(alt. Antonella, Antonina)

Latin, meaning 'invaluable'.

Anwen
Welsh, meaning 'very fair'.

Anya
(alt. Aniya, Aniyah, Aniylah, Anja)

Russian, meaning 'grace'.

Apollonia
Feminine of Apollo, the Greek god of the sun.

Apple
From the name of the fruit.

April
(alt. Avril)

Latin, meaning 'opening up'. Also the name of the month.

Aquilina
(alt. Aqua, Aquila)

Spanish, meaning 'like an eagle'.

Ara
Arabic, meaning 'brings rain'.

Arabella
Latin, meaning 'answered prayer'.

Araceli
(alt. Aracely)

Spanish, meaning 'altar of Heaven'.

A

Araminta

Contraction of Arabella and Amita, meaning 'altar of Heaven' and 'friendship'.

Arcadia

Greek, meaning 'paradise'.

Ardelle
(alt. Ardell, Ardella)

Latin, meaning 'burning with enthusiasm'.

Arden
(alt. Ardis, Ardith)

Latin, meaning 'burning with enthusiasm'.

Arella
(alt. Areli, Arely)

Hebrew, meaning 'angel'.

Aretha

Greek, meaning 'woman of virtue'.

Aria
(alt. Ariah)

Italian, meaning 'melody'.

Ariadne

Both Greek and Latin, meaning 'the very holy one'. In Greek mythology, Ariadne was the daughter of King Minos.

Ariana
(alt. Ariane, Arianna, Arienne)

Welsh, meaning 'silver'.

Ariel
(alt. Ariela, Ariella, Arielle)

Hebrew, meaning 'lioness of God'.

Arlene
(alt. Arleen, Arlie, Arline, Arly)

Gaelic, meaning 'pledge'.

Armida

Latin, meaning 'little armed one'.

Artemisia
(alt. Artemis)

Greek/Spanish, meaning 'perfect'.

Artie
(alt. Arti)

Shortened form of Artemisia, meaning 'perfect'.

Ashanti

Geographical area in Africa

Ashby

English, meaning 'ash tree farm'.

Ashley

(alt. Ashlee, Ashleigh, Ashli, Ashlie, Ashly)

English, meaning 'ash tree meadow'.

Ashlynn

(alt. Ashlyn)

Irish Gaelic, meaning 'dream'.

Ashton

(alt. Ashtyn)

Old English, meaning 'ash tree town'.

Asia

Name of the continent.

Asma

(alt. Asmara)

Arabic, meaning 'high-standing'.

Aspen

(alt. Aspynn)

Name of the tree. Also name of a city in the US.

Assumpta

(alt. Assunta)

Italian, meaning 'raised up'.

Asta

(alt. Asteria, Astor, Astoria)

Greek or Latin, meaning 'star-like'.

Astrid

Old Norse, meaning 'beautiful like a God'.

Atara

Hebrew, meaning 'diadem'.

Athena

(alt. Athenais)

The Greek goddess of wisdom.

Aubrey

(alt. Aubree, Aubriana, Aubrie)

French, meaning 'elf ruler'.

Audrey
(alt. Audra, Audrie, Audrina, Audry)

English, meaning 'noble strength'.

Augusta
(alt. August, Augustine)

Latin, meaning 'worthy of respect'.

Aura
(alt. Aurea)

Greek or Latin, meaning either 'soft breeze' or 'gold'.

Aurelia
(alt. Aurelie)

Latin, meaning gold.

Aurora
(alt. Aurore)

In Roman mythology, Aurora was the goddess of sunrise.

Austine
(alt. Austen, Austin)

Latin, meaning 'worthy of respect'.

Autumn
Name of the season.

Ava
(alt. Avia, Avie)

Latin, meaning 'like a bird'.

Avalon
(alt. Avalyn, Aveline)

Celtic, meaning 'island of apples'.

Axelle
Greek, meaning 'father of peace'.

Aya
(alt. Ayah)

Hebrew, meaning 'bird'.

Ayanna
(alt. Ayana)

American, meaning 'grace'.

Ayesha
(alt. Aisha, Aysha)

Persian, meaning 'small one'.

Azalea
Latin, meaning 'dry earth'.

A

Azalia

Hebrew, meaning 'aided by God'.

Aziza

Hebrew, meaning 'mighty', or Arabic meaning 'precious'.

Azure

(alt. Azaria)

French, meaning 'sky-blue'.

Popular French names for boys and girls

Adele
Alain
Alphonse
Belle
Fleur
Jacques
Marc
Matthieu
Paulette
Sabine

B Girls' names

Babette
(alt. Babe)

French version of Barbara, Greek meaning 'foreign'.

Bailey
(alt. Baeli, Bailee)

English, meaning 'law enforcer'.

Bambi

Shortened version of the Italian Bambina, meaning 'child'.

Barbara
(alt. Barb, Barbie, Barbra)

Greek, meaning 'foreign'.

Basma

Arabic, meaning 'smile'.

Bathsheba

Hebrew, meaning 'daughter of the oath'.

Bay
(alt. Baya)

Plant or geographical name.

Beata

Latin, meaning 'blessed'.

Beatrice
(alt. Beatrix, Beatriz, Bellatrix)

Latin, meaning 'bringer of gladness'.

Becky
(alt. Beccie, Beccy, Beckie)

Shortened form of Rebecca, Hebrew meaning 'joined'.

B

Literary names

Alice (*Alice in Wonderland*, Lewis Carroll)
Beth (*Little Women*, Louisa M Alcott)
Cora (*Last of the Mohicans*, James Fenimore Cooper)
Eliza (*Pygmalion*, George Bernard Shaw)
Gwendolen (*The Importance of Being Earnest*, Oscar Wilde)
Hermione (Harry Potter series, J K Rowling)
Isabella (Twilight series, Stephenie Meyer)
Matilda (*Matilda*, Roald Dahl)
Miranda (*The Tempest*, William Shakespeare)
Wendy (*Peter Pan*, J M Barrie)

Bee

Shortened form of Beatrice, meaning 'bringer of gladness'.

Belinda

(alt. Belen, Belina)

Contraction of Belle and Linda, meaning 'beautiful'.

Bell

Shortened form of Isabel, meaning 'pledged to God'.

Bella

Latin, meaning 'beautiful'.

Belle

French, meaning 'beautiful'.

Belva

Latin, meaning 'beautiful view'.

Bénédicta

Latin, the feminine of Benedict, meaning 'blessed'.

Benita

(alt. Bernita)

Spanish, meaning 'blessed'.

Bennie

Shortened version of Bénédicta and Benita.

B

Berit
(alt. Beret)
Scandinavian, meaning 'splendid' or 'gorgeous'.

Bernadette
French, meaning 'courageous'.

Bernadine
French, meaning 'courageous'.

Bernice
(alt. Berenice, Berniece, Burnice)
Greek, meaning 'she who brings victory'.

Bertha
(alt. Berta, Berthe, Bertie)
German, meaning 'bright'.

Beryl
Greek, meaning 'pale, green gemstone'.

Bess
(alt. Bessie)
Shortened form of Elizabeth, meaning 'consecrated to God'.

Beth
Hebrew, meaning 'house'. Also shortened form of Elizabeth, meaning 'consecrated to God'.

Bethany
(alt. Bethan)
Hebrew, referring to a geographical location.

Bethel
Hebrew, meaning 'house of God'.

Bettina
Spanish version of Elizabeth, meaning 'consecrated to God'.

Betty
(alt. Betsy, Bette, Bettie, Bettye)
Shortened version of Elizabeth, meaning 'consecrated to God'.

Beulah
Hebrew, meaning 'married'.

Beverly
(alt. Beverlee, Beverley)
English, meaning 'beaver stream'.

B

Beyoncé

American, made popular by the singer.

Bianca

(alt. Blanca)

Italian, meaning 'white'.

Bijou

French, meaning 'precious ring'.

Billie

(alt. Bill, Billy, Billye)

Shortened version of Wilhelmina, meaning 'determined'.

Bina

Hebrew, meaning 'knowledge'.

Birgit

(alt. Birgitta)

Norwegian, meaning 'splendid'.

Blair

Scottish Gaelic, meaning 'flat, plain area'.

Blake

(alt. Blakely, Blakelyn)

English, meaning either 'pale-skinned' or 'dark'.

Blanche

(alt. Blanch)

French, meaning 'white or pale'.

Bliss

English, meaning 'intense happiness'.

Blithe

English, meaning 'joyous'.

Blodwen

Welsh, meaning 'white flower'.

Blossom

English, meaning 'flowerlike'.

Blythe

(alt. Bly)

English, meaning 'happy and carefree'.

Bobbi

(alt. Bobbie, Bobby)

Shortened version of Roberta, meaning 'bright fame'.

B

Bonita
Spanish, meaning 'pretty'.

Bonnie
(alt. Bonny)
Scottish, meaning 'fair of face'.

Brandy
(alt. Brandee, Brandi, Brandie)
Name of the liquor.

Brea
(alt. Bree, Bria)
Shortened form of Brianna, meaning 'strong'.

Brenda
English, meaning 'burning or stinking hair'.

Brianna
(alt. Breana, Breann, Breanna, Breanne, Brenna, Brenyn, Briana, Brianne, Bryanna)
Irish Gaelic, meaning 'strong'.

Bridget
(alt. Bridgett, Bridgette, Brigette, Brigid, Brigitta, Brigitte)
Irish Gaelic, meaning 'strength and power'.

Brier
French, meaning 'heather'.

Brit
(alt. Britt, Britta)
Celtic, meaning 'spotted' or 'freckled'.

Britannia
Latin, meaning 'Britain'.

Brittany
(alt. Britany, Britney, Britni, Brittani, Brittanie, Brittney, Brittni, Brittny)
Latin, meaning 'from England'.

Biblical names

Elizabeth
Eve
Hannah
Leah
Mary
Miriam
Rachel
Rebecca
Ruth
Sarah

B

Bronwyn
(alt. Bronwen)

Welsh, meaning 'fair breast'.

Brooke
(alt. Brook)

English, meaning 'small stream'.

Brooklyn
(alt. Brooklynn)

Name of a New York borough.

Brunhilda

German, meaning 'armor-wearing fighting maid'.

Bryn
(alt. Brynn)

Welsh, meaning 'mount'.

Bryony
(alt. Briony)

Name of a European vine.

Popular Indian names for boys and girls

Ajay
Bharat
Deepal
Haresh
Jaya
Manisha
Paresh
Rabiya
Ravi
Sunita

B

C Girls' names

Cadence
Latin, meaning 'with rhythm'.

Cai
Vietnamese, meaning 'feminine'.

Caitlin
(alt. Cadyn, Caitlann, Caitlyn, Caitlynn)
Greek, meaning 'pure'.

Calandra
Greek, meaning 'lark'.

Calantha
(alt. Calanthe)
Greek, meaning 'lovely flower'.

Caledonia
Latin, meaning 'from Scotland'.

Calla
Greek, meaning 'beautiful'.

Callie
(alt. Caleigh, Cali, Calleigh, Cally)
Greek, meaning 'beauty'.

Calliope
Greek, meaning 'beautiful voice'. From the muse of epic poetry in Greek mythology.

Callista
(alt. Callisto)
Greek, meaning 'most beautiful'.

Camas

Native American, from the root and bulb of the same name.

Cambria

Welsh, from the alternative name for Wales.

Camden
(alt. Camdyn)

English, meaning 'winding valley'.

Cameo

Italian, meaning 'skin'.

Cameron
(alt. Camryn)

Scottish Gaelic, meaning 'bent nose'.

Camilla
(alt. Camelia, Camellia, Camila, Camillia)

Latin, meaning 'spiritual serving girl'.

Camille

Latin, meaning 'spiritual serving girl'.

Candace
(alt. Candice, Candis)

Latin, meaning 'brilliant white'.

Candida

Latin, meaning 'white'.

Candra

Latin, meaning 'glowing'.

Candy
(alt. Candi)

Shortened form of Candace, meaning 'brilliant white'.

Caoimhe

Celtic, meaning 'gentleness'.

Caprice

Italian, meaning 'ruled by whim'.

Cara

Latin, meaning 'darling'.

Caren
(alt. Carin, Caron, Caryn)

Greek, meaning 'pure'.

C

Carey

(alt. Cari, Carie, Carri, Carrie, Cary)

Welsh, meaning 'near the castle'.

Carina

(alt. Corina)

Italian, meaning 'dearest little one'.

Carissa

(alt. Carisa)

Greek, meaning 'grace'.

Carla

(alt. Charla)

Feminine of the Old Norse Carl, meaning 'free man'.

Carlin

(alt. Carleen, Carlene)

Gaelic, meaning 'little champion'.

Carlotta

(alt. Carlota)

Italian, meaning 'free man'.

Carly

(alt. Carlee, Carley, Carli, Carlie)

Feminine of the German Charles, meaning 'man'.

Carmel

(alt. Carmela, Carmelita, Carmella)

Hebrew, meaning 'garden'.

Carmen

(alt. Carma, Carmina)

Latin, meaning 'song'.

Carol

(alt. Carole, Carrol, Carroll, Caryl)

Shortened form of Caroline, meaning 'man'.

Caroline

(alt. Carolann, Carolina, Carolyn, Carolynn)

German, meaning 'man'.

Carrington

English, meaning 'Charles's town'.

Carys

(alt. Cerys)

Welsh, meaning 'love'.

Casey

(alt. Casy, Casie)

Irish Gaelic, meaning 'watchful'.

C

Saints' names

Ada
Agatha
Catherine
Felicity
Helena
Joan
Lydia
Margaret
Mary
Teresa

Cassandra
(alt. Casandra, Cassandre)
Greek, meaning 'one who prophesies doom'.

Cassia
(alt. Casia, Casie, Cassie)
Greek, meaning 'cinnamon'.

Cassidy
Irish, meaning 'clever'.

Catalina
(alt. Catarina, Caterina)
Spanish version of Catherine, meaning 'pure'.

Catherine
(alt. Catharine, Cathrine, Cathryn)
Greek, meaning 'pure'.

Cathleen
Irish version of Catherine, meaning 'pure'.

Cathy
(alt. Cathey, Cathi, Cathie)
Shortened form of Catherine, meaning 'pure'.

Caty
(alt. Caddie, Caitee, Cate, Catie)
Shortened form of Catherine, meaning 'pure'.

Cayley
(alt. Cayla, Caylee, Caylen)
American, meaning 'pure'.

Cecilia
(alt. Cecelia, Cecily, Cicely, Cicily)
Latin, meaning 'blind one'.

Cecile
(alt. Cecilie)
Latin, meaning 'blind one'.

C

Celena

Greek, meaning 'goddess of the moon'.

Celeste

(alt. Celestina, Celestine)

Latin, meaning 'heavenly'.

Celine

(alt. Celia, Celina)

French version of Celeste, meaning 'heavenly'.

Cerise

French, meaning 'cherry'.

Chanah

Hebrew, meaning 'grace'.

Chance

Middle English, meaning 'good fortune'.

Chandler

(alt. Chandell)

English, meaning 'candle maker'.

Chandra

(alt. Chanda, Chandry)

Sanskrit, meaning 'like the moon'.

Chanel

(alt. Chanelle)

French, from the designer of the same name.

Chantal

(alt. Chantel, Chantelle, Chantilly)

French, meaning 'stony spot'.

Chardonnay

French, from the wine variety of the same name.

Charis

(alt. Charice, Charissa, Charisse)

Greek, meaning 'grace'.

Charity

Latin, meaning 'brotherly love'.

Charlene

(alt. Charleen, Charline)

German, meaning 'man'.

Charlie

(alt. Charlee, Charley, Charlize, Charly)

Shortened form of Charlotte, meaning 'little and feminine'.

C

Charlotte
(alt. Charnette, Charolette)
French, meaning 'little and feminine'.

Charmaine
Latin, meaning 'clan'.

Chastity
Latin, meaning 'purity'.

Chava
(alt. Chaya)
Hebrew, meaning 'beloved'.

Chelsea
(alt. Chelsee, Chelsey, Chelsi, Chelsie)
English, meaning 'port or landing place'.

Cher
French, meaning 'beloved'.

Cherie
(alt. Cheri, Cherise)
French, meaning 'dear'.

Cherish
(alt. Cherith)
English, meaning 'to treasure'.

Chermona
Hebrew, meaning 'sacred mountain'.

Cherry
(alt. Cherri)
French, meaning 'cherry fruit'.

TV personality names

Cat (Deeley)
Connie (Chung)
Ellen (DeGeneres)
Giada (De Laurentiis)
Giuliana (Rancic)
Mary (Hart)
Oprah (Winfrey)
Padma (Lakshmi)
Samantha (Harris)
Tyra (Banks)

C

Cheryl
(alt. Cheryle)

English, meaning 'little and womanly'.

Chesney

English, meaning 'place to camp'.

Cheyenne
(alt. Cheyanne)

Native American, from the tribe of the same name.

Chiara
(alt. Ceara, Chiarina, Ciara)

Italian, meaning 'light'.

China

From the country of the same name.

Chiquita

Spanish, meaning 'little one'.

Chloe
(alt. Cloe)

Greek, meaning 'pale green shoot'.

Chloris

Greek, meaning 'pale'.

Chris
(alt. Chrissy, Christa, Christie, Christy, Crissy, Cristy)

Shortened form of Christina, meaning 'anointed Christian'.

Christabel

Latin and French, meaning 'fair Christian'.

Christina
(alt. Christiana, Cristina)

Greek, meaning 'anointed Christian'.

Christine
(alt. Christeen, Christen, Christene, Christian, Christiane, Christin)

Greek, meaning 'anointed Christian'.

Chuma

Aramaic, meaning 'warmth'.

Cierra
(alt. Ciera)

Irish, meaning 'black'.

Cinderella

French, meaning 'little ash-girl'.

C

Cindy
(alt. Cinda, Cindi, Cyndi)

Shortened form of Cynthia, meaning 'goddess'.

Cinnamon

Greek, from the spice of the same name.

Citlali
(alt. Citlalli)

Aztec, meaning 'star'.

Citrine

Latin, from the gemstone of the same name.

Claire
(alt. Clare)

Latin, meaning 'bright'.

Clara
(alt. Claira)

Latin, meaning 'bright'.

Clarabelle
(alt. Claribel)

Contraction of Clara and Isobel, meaning 'bright' and 'consecrated to God'.

Clarissa
(alt. Clarice, Clarisse)

Variation of Claire, meaning 'bright'.

Clarity

Latin, meaning 'lucid'.

Claudette

Latin, meaning 'lame'.

Claudia
(alt. Claudie, Claudine)

Latin, meaning 'lame'.

Clematis

Greek, meaning 'vine'.

Clementine
(alt. Clemency, Clementina, Clemmie)

Latin, meaning 'mild and merciful'.

Cleopatra

Greek, meaning 'her father's renown'.

Clio
(alt. Cleo, Cliona)

Greek, from the muse of history of the same name.

C

Clodagh
Irish, meaning 'river'.

Clotilda
(alt. Clothilda, Clothilde, Clotilde)
German, meaning 'renowned battle'.

Clover
English, from the flower of the same name.

Coco
Spanish, meaning 'help'.

Cody
English, meaning 'pillow'.

Colleen
(alt. Coleen)
Irish Gaelic, meaning 'girl'.

Collette
(alt. Colette)
Greek/French, meaning 'people of victory'.

Connie
Latin, meaning 'steadfast'.

Constance
(alt. Constanza)
Latin, meaning 'steadfast'.

Consuelo
(alt. Consuela)
Spanish, meaning 'comfort'.

Cora
Greek, meaning 'maiden'.

Coral
(alt. Coralie, Coraline, Corelia, Corene)
Latin, from the marine life of the same name.

Corazon
Spanish, meaning 'heart'.

Cordelia
(alt. Cordia, Cordie)
Latin, meaning 'heart'.

Corey
(alt. Cori, Corrie, Cory)
Irish Gaelic, meaning 'the hollow'.

Corin
(alt. Corine)
Latin, meaning 'spear'.

Corinne
(alt. Corinna, Corrine)
French version of Cora, meaning 'maiden'.

C

Corliss
English, meaning 'cheery'.

Cornelia
Latin, meaning 'like a horn'.

Cosette
French, meaning 'people of victory'.

Cosima
(alt. Cosmina)
Greek, meaning 'order'.

Courtney
(alt. Cortney)
English, meaning 'court-dweller'.

Creola
French, meaning 'American-born, English descent'.

Crescent
French, meaning 'increasing'.

Cressida
From the heroine in Greek mythology of the same name.

Crystal
(alt. Christal, Chrystal, Cristal)
Greek, meaning 'ice'.

Csilla
Hungarian, meaning 'defences'.

Cynara
Greek, meaning 'thistly plant'.

Cynthia
Greek, meaning 'goddess from the mountain'.

Cyra
Persian, meaning 'sun'.

Cyrilla
Latin, meaning 'lordly'.

C

D

Girls' names

Dacey
Irish Gaelic, meaning 'from the south'.

Dada
Nigerian, meaning 'curly haired'.

Dagmar
German, meaning 'day's glory'.

Dagny
Nordic, meaning 'new day'.

Dahlia
Scandinavian, from the flower of the same name.

Dai
Japanese, meaning 'great'.

Daisy
(alt. Dasia)
English, meaning 'eye of the day'.

Dakota
Native American, meaning 'allies'.

Dalia
(alt. Dalila)
Hebrew, meaning 'delicate branch'.

Dallas
Scottish Gaelic, from the village of the same name. Also a city in Texas.

Damaris
Greek, meaning 'calf'.

Damita

Spanish, meaning 'little noblewoman'.

Dana

(alt. Dania, Danna, Dayna)

English, meaning 'from Denmark'.

Danae

Greek, from the mythological heroine of the same name.

Danica

(alt. Danika)

Latin, meaning 'from Denmark'.

Danielle

(alt. Danelle, Daniela, Daniella, Danila, Danyelle)

The feminine form of the Hebrew Daniel, meaning 'God is my judge'.

Danita

English, meaning 'God will judge'.

Daphne

(alt. Dafne, Daphna)

Greek, meaning 'laurel tree'.

Dara

Hebrew/Persian, meaning 'wisdom'.

Darby

(alt. Darbi, Darbie)

Irish, meaning 'park with deer'.

Darcie

(alt. Darci, Darcy)

Irish Gaelic, meaning 'dark'.

Daria

Greek, meaning 'rich'.

Darla

English, meaning 'darling'.

Darlene

(alt. Darleen, Darline)

American, meaning 'darling'.

Daryl

(alt. Darryl)

English, originally used as a last name.

Davina

Hebrew, meaning 'loved one'.

Dawn

(alt. Dawna)

English, meaning 'the dawn'.

D

Daya

Hebrew, meaning 'bird of prey'.

Deanna

(alt. Dayana, Deana, Deanna, Deanne)

English, meaning 'valley'.

Debbie

(alt. Debbi, Debby, Debi)

Shortened form of Deborah, meaning 'bee'.

Deborah

(alt. Debbra, Debora, Debra, Debrah)

Hebrew, meaning 'bee'.

December

Latin, meaning 'tenth month'.

Dee

Welsh, meaning 'swarthy'.

Deidre

(alt. Deidra, Deirdre)

Irish, meaning 'raging woman'.

Deja

(alt. Dejah)

French, meaning 'already'.

Delaney

Irish Gaelic, meaning 'offspring of the challenger'.

Delia

Greek, meaning 'from Delos'.

Delilah

(alt. Delina)

Hebrew, meaning 'seductive'.

Della

(alt. Dell)

Shortened form of Adele, meaning 'nobility'.

Delores

(alt. Deloris)

Spanish, meaning 'sorrows'.

Delphine

(alt. Delpha, Delphia, Delphina, Delphinia)

Greek, meaning 'dolphin'.

Delta

Greek, meaning 'fourth child'.

Demetria

(alt. Demetrice, Dimitria)

Greek, from the mythological heroine of the same name.

Demi

French, meaning 'half'.

Dena

(alt. Deena)

English, meaning 'from the valley'.

Denise

(alt. Denice, Denisa, Denisse)

French, meaning 'follower of Dionysius'.

Desdemona

Greek, meaning 'wretchedness'.

Desiree

(alt. Desirae)

French, meaning 'much desired'.

Desma

Greek, meaning 'blinding oath'.

Destiny

(alt. Destany, Destinee, Destiney, Destini)

French, meaning 'fate'.

Deva

Hindi, meaning 'God-like'.

Devin

(alt. Devinne)

Irish Gaelic, meaning 'poet'.

Devon

English, from the county of the same name.

Diamond

English, meaning 'brilliant'.

Diana

(alt. Dian, Diane, Dianna, Dianne)

Roman, meaning 'divine'.

Diandra

Greek, meaning 'two males'.

Dilys

Welsh, meaning 'reliable'.

Dimona

Hebrew, meaning 'south'.

Dinah

(alt. Dina)

Hebrew, meaning 'justified'.

Dionne

Greek, from the mythological heroine of the same name.

D

Uncommon three syllable names

Annabel	India
Cassandra	Priscilla
Evelyn	Tamara
Gloria	Vanessa
Harriet	

Divine
Italian, meaning 'heavenly'.

Dixie
French, meaning 'tenth'.

Dodie
Hebrew, meaning 'well-loved'.

Dolly
(alt. Dollie)
Shortened form of Dorothy, meaning 'gift of 'God'.

Dolores
(alt. Doloris)
Spanish, meaning 'sorrows'.

Dominique
(alt. Domenica, Dominica, Domonique)
Latin, meaning 'Lord'.

Donata
Latin, meaning 'given'.

Donna
(alt. Dona, Donnie)
Italian, meaning 'lady'.

Dora
Greek, meaning 'gift'.

Dorcas
Greek, meaning 'gazelle'.

Doreen
(alt. Dorene, Dorine)
Irish Gaelic, meaning 'brooding'.

Doris
(alt. Dorris)
Greek, from the place of the same name.

D

Dorothy
(alt. Dorathy, Doretha, Dorotha, Dorothea, Dorthy)
Greek, meaning 'gift of God'.

Dorrit
(alt. Dorit)
Greek, meaning 'gift of God'.

Dory
(alt. Dori)
French, meaning 'gilded'.

Dottie
(alt. Dotty)
Shortened form of Dorothy, meaning 'gift of God'.

Dove
(alt. Dovie)
English, from the bird of the same name.

Drew
Greek, meaning 'masculine'.

Drusilla
(alt. Drucilla)
Latin, meaning 'of the Drusus clan'.

Dulcie
(alt. Dulce, Dulcia)
Latin, meaning 'sweet'.

Dusty
(alt. Dusti)
English, from the place of the same name.

D

E Girls' names

Earla
English, meaning 'leader'.

Eartha
English, meaning 'earth'.

Easter
Egyptian, from the festival of the same name.

Ebba
English, meaning 'fortress of riches'.

Ebony
(alt. Eboni)
Latin, meaning 'deep, black wood'.

Echo
Greek, meaning 'reflected sound'. From the mythological nymph of the same name.

Eda
(alt. Edda)
English, meaning 'wealthy and happy'.

Edelmira
Spanish, meaning 'admired for nobility'.

Eden
Hebrew, meaning 'pleasure'.

Edie
(alt. Eddie)
Shortened form of Eden, meaning 'pleasure'.

E

Edina

Scottish, meaning 'from Edinburgh'.

Edith

(alt. Edyth)

English, meaning 'prosperity through battle'.

Edna

Hebrew, meaning 'enjoyment'.

Edrea

English, meaning 'wealthy and powerful'.

Edwina

English, meaning 'wealthy friend'.

Effie

Greek, meaning 'pleasant speech'.

Eglantine

French, from the shrub of the same name.

Eibhlín

Irish Gaelic, meaning 'shining and brilliant'.

Eileen

Irish, meaning 'shining and brilliant'.

Ekaterina

(alt. Ekaterini)

Slavic, meaning 'pure'.

Elaine

(alt. Elaina, Elayne)

French, meaning 'bright, shining light'.

Elba

Italian, from the island of the same name.

Elberta

English, meaning 'high-born'.

Eldora

Spanish, meaning 'covered with gold'.

Eleanor

(alt. Elana, Elanor, Eleanora, Eleanore, Elena, Eleni, Elenor, Elenora, Elina, Elinor, Elinore)

Greek, meaning 'light'.

Electra
(alt. Elektra)
Greek, meaning 'shining', also from the myth.

Elfrida
(alt. Elfrieda)
English, meaning 'elf power'.

Eliane
Hebrew, meaning 'Jehovah is God'.

Elissa
(alt. Elisa)
French, meaning 'pledged to God'.

Eliza
(alt. Elisha)
Hebrew, meaning 'pledged to God'.

Elizabeth
(alt. Elisabet, Elisabeth, Elizabella, Elsbeth, Elspeth)
Hebrew, meaning 'pledged to God'.

Elke
German, meaning 'nobility'.

Ella
German, meaning 'completely'.

Elle
(alt. Ellie)
French, meaning 'she'.

Ellen
(alt. Elin, Eline, Ellyn)
Greek, meaning 'shining'.

Ellice
(alt. Elyse)
Greek, meaning 'the Lord is God'.

Elma
(alt. Elna)
Latin, meaning 'soul'.

Elmira
Arabic, meaning 'aristocratic lady'.

Elodie
French, meaning 'marsh flower'.

Eloise
(alt. Elois, Eloisa, Elouise)
French, meaning 'renowned in battle'.

E

Elsa
(alt. Else, Elsie)
Hebrew, meaning 'pledged to God'.

Elula
Hebrew, meaning 'August'.

Elva
Irish, meaning 'noble'.

Elvina
English, meaning 'noble friend'.

Elvira
(alt. Elvera)
Spanish, from the place of the same name.

Ember
(alt. Embry)
English, meaning 'spark'.

Emeline
German, meaning 'industrious'.

Emerald
English, meaning 'green gemstone'.

Emery
German, meaning 'ruler of work'.

Emilia
Latin, meaning 'rival, eager'.

Emily
(alt. Emelie, Emilee, Emilie, Emlyn)
Latin, meaning 'rival, eager'.

Emma
German, meaning 'embraces everything'.

Emmanuelle
Hebrew, meaning 'God is among us'.

Emmeline
(alt. Emmelina)
German, meaning 'embraces everything'.

Emmy
(alt. Emi, Emme, Emmie)
German, meaning 'embraces everything'.

Ena
Shortened form of Georgina, meaning 'farmer'.

Enid
(alt. Eneida)
Welsh, meaning 'life spirit'.

E

Enola

Native American, meaning 'solitary'.

Enya

Irish Gaelic, meaning 'fire'.

Erica

(alt. Ericka, Erika)

Scandinavian, meaning 'ruler forever'.

Erin

(alt. Eryn)

Irish Gaelic, meaning 'from the isle to the west'.

Eris

Greek, from the mythological heroine of the same name.

Erlinda

Hebrew, meaning 'spirited'.

Erma

German, meaning 'universal'.

Ermine

French, meaning 'weasel'.

Erna

English, meaning 'sincere'.

Ernestine

(alt. Ernestina)

English, meaning 'sincere'.

Esme

French, meaning 'esteemed'.

Esmeralda

Spanish, meaning 'emerald'.

Esperanza

Spanish, meaning 'hope'.

Estelle

(alt. Estela, Estell, Estella)

French, meaning 'star'.

Esther

(alt. Esta, Ester, Etha, Ethna, Ethne)

Persian, meaning 'star'.

Eternity

Latin, meaning 'forever'.

Ethel

(alt. Ethyl)

English, meaning 'noble'.

Etta

(alt. Etter, Ettie)

Shortened form of Henrietta, meaning 'ruler of the house'.

E

Eudora
Greek, meaning 'generous gift'.

Eugenia
(alt. Eugenie)
Greek, meaning 'well born'.

Eulalia
(alt. Eula, Eulah, Eulalie)
Greek, meaning 'sweet-speaking'.

Eunice
Greek, meaning 'victorious'.

Euphemia
Greek, meaning ' favorable speech'.

Eva
Hebrew, meaning 'life'.

Evadne
Greek, meaning 'pleasing one'.

Evangeline
(alt. Evangelina)
Greek, meaning 'good news'.

Evanthe
Greek, meaning 'good flower'.

Eve
(alt. Evie)
Hebrew, meaning 'life'.

Evelina
(alt. Evelia)
German, meaning 'hazelnut'.

Evelyn
(alt. Evalyn, Evelin, Eveline, Evelyne)
German, meaning 'hazelnut'.

Everly
(alt. Everleigh, Everley)
English, meaning 'grazing meadow'.

Evette
French, meaning 'yew wood'.

Evonne
(alt. Evon)
French, meaning 'yew wood'.

E

F
Girls' names

Fabia
(alt. Fabiana, Fabienne, Fabiola, Fabriana)
Latin, meaning 'from the Fabian clan'.

Fabrizia
Italian, meaning 'works with hands'.

Faith
English, meaning 'loyalty'.

Faiza
Arabic, meaning 'victorious'.

Fallon
Irish Gaelic, meaning 'descended from a ruler'.

Fanny
(alt. Fannie)
Latin, meaning 'from France'.

Farica
German, meaning 'peaceful ruler'.

Farrah
English, meaning 'lovely and pleasant'.

Fatima
Arabic, meaning 'baby's nurse'.

Faustine
Latin, meaning 'fortunate'.

Fawn
French, meaning 'young deer'.

F

Fay
(alt. Fae, Faye)
French, meaning 'fairy'.

Felicia
(alt. Felecia, Felice, Felicita, Felisha)
Latin, meaning 'lucky and happy'.

Felicity
Latin, meaning 'fortunate'.

Fenella
Irish Gaelic, meaning 'white shoulder'.

Old name, new fashion?

Bella
Carolyn
Clara
Dorothy
Emmeline
Hazel
Matilda
Nora
Penelope
Rosalie

Fenia
Scandinavian, from the mythological giantess of the same name.

Fern
(alt. Ferne, Ferrin)
English, from the plant of the same name.

Fernanda
German, meaning 'peace and courage'.

Ffion
(alt. Fion)
Irish Gaelic, meaning 'fair and pale'.

Fia
Italian, meaning 'flame'.

Fifi
Hebrew, meaning 'Jehovah increases'.

Filomena
Greek, meaning 'loved one'.

F

Finlay
(alt. Finley)

Irish Gaelic, meaning 'fair-headed courageous one'.

Finola
(alt. Fionnula)

Irish Gaelic, meaning 'fair shoulder'.

Fiona

Irish Gaelic, meaning 'fair and pale'.

Fiora

Irish Gaelic, meaning 'fair and pale'.

Flanna
(alt. Flannery)

Irish Gaelic, meaning 'russet hair'.

Flavia

Latin, meaning 'yellow hair'.

Fleur

French, meaning 'flower'.

Flo
(alt. Florrie, Flossie, Floy)

Shortened form of Florence, meaning 'in bloom'.

Flora

Latin, meaning 'flower'.

Florence
(alt. Florencia, Florene, Florine)

Latin, meaning 'in bloom'.

Florida

Latin, meaning 'flowery'. Also a state in America.

Fran
(alt. Frankie, Frannie)

Shortened form of Frances, meaning 'from France'.

Frances
(alt. Francine, Francis)

Latin, meaning 'from France'.

Francesca
(alt. Franchesca, Francisca)

Latin, meaning 'from France'.

F

Freda

(alt. Freida, Frida, Frieda)

German, meaning 'peaceful'.

Frederica

German, meaning 'peaceful ruler'.

Fuchsia

German, from the flower of the same name.

Names of poets

Adrienne (Rich)
Anne (Sexton)
Carol Ann (Duffy)
Charlotte (Perkins Gilman)
Emily (Dickinson)
Erica (Jong)
Maya (Angelou)
Pam (Ayres)
Sylvia (Plath)
Wendy (Cope)

F

G Girls' names

Gabby
(alt. Gabbi)
Shortened form of Gabrielle, meaning 'heroine of God'.

Gabrielle
(alt. Gabriel, Gabriela, Gabriella)
Hebrew, meaning 'heroine of God'.

Gaia
(alt. Gaea)
Greek, meaning 'the earth'.

Gail
(alt. Gale, Gayla, Gayle)
Hebrew, meaning 'my father rejoices'.

Gala
French, meaning 'festive merrymaking'.

Galiena
German, meaning 'high one'.

Galina
Russian, meaning 'shining brightly'.

Garnet
(alt. Garnett)
English, meaning 'red gemstone'.

Gay
(alt. Gaye)
French, meaning 'glad and lighthearted'.

Gaynor
Welsh, meaning 'white and smooth'.

Gemini
Greek, meaning 'twin'.

Gemma
Italian, meaning 'precious stone'.

Gene
Greek, meaning 'well born'.

Genesis
Greek, meaning 'beginning'.

Geneva
(alt. Genevra)
French, meaning 'juniper tree'.

Genevieve
German, meaning 'white wave'.

Genie
Shortened form of Genevieve, meaning 'white wave'.

Georgette
French, meaning 'farmer'.

Names from ancient Rome

Aggripina
Antonia
Claudia
Drusilla
Honorata
Hortensia
Narcissa
Romana
Tatiana
Valeria

Georgia
(alt. Georgiana, Georgianna, Georgie)
Latin, meaning 'farmer'.

Georgina
(alt. Georgene, Georgine, Giorgina)
Latin, meaning 'farmer'.

Geraldine
German, meaning 'spear ruler'.

Gerda
Nordic, meaning 'shelter'.

Geri
(alt. Gerri, Gerry)
Shortened form of Geraldine, meaning 'spear ruler'.

Germaine
French, meaning 'from Germany'.

Gertie
Shortened form of Gertrude, meaning 'strength of a spear'.

Gertrude
German, meaning 'strength of a spear'.

Gia
(alt. Ghia)
Italian, meaning 'God is gracious'.

Gianina
(alt. Giana)
Hebrew, meaning 'God's graciousness'.

Gigi
(alt. Giget)
Shortened form of Georgina, meaning 'farmer'.

Gilda
English, meaning 'gilded'.

Gilia
Hebrew, meaning 'joy of the Lord'.

Gillian
Latin, meaning 'youthful'.

Gina
(alt. Geena, Gena)
Shortened form of Regina, meaning 'queen'.

Ginger
Latin, from the root of the same name.

Ginny
Shortened form of Virginia, meaning 'virgin'.

Giovanna
Italian, meaning 'God is gracious'.

Giselle
(alt. Gisela, Gisele, Giselle, Gisselle)
German, meaning 'pledge'.

G

Gita
(alt. Geeta)

Sanskrit, meaning 'song'.

Giulia
(alt. Giuliana)

Italian, meaning 'youthful'.

Gladys
(alt. Gladyce)

Welsh, meaning 'lame'.

Glenda

Welsh, meaning 'fair and good'.

Glenna
(alt. Glennie)

Irish Gaelic, meaning 'glen'.

Gloria
(alt. Glory)

Latin, meaning 'glory'.

Glynda
(alt. Glinda)

Welsh, meaning 'fair'.

Glynis

Welsh, meaning 'small glen'.

Golda
(alt. Goldia, Goldie)

English, meaning 'gold'.

Grace
(alt. Graça, Gracie, Gracin, Grayce)

Latin, meaning 'grace'.

Grainne
(alt. Grania)

Irish Gaelic, meaning 'love'.

Gratia
(alt. Grasia)

Latin, meaning 'blessing'.

Greer
(alt. Grier)

Latin, meaning 'alert and watchful'.

Gregoria

Latin, meaning 'alert'.

Greta
(alt. Gretel)

Greek, meaning 'pearl'.

G

Gretchen

German, meaning 'pearl'.

Griselda

(alt. Griselle)

German, meaning 'gray fighting maid'.

Gudrun

Scandinavian, meaning 'battle'.

Guinevere

Welsh, meaning 'white and smooth'.

Gwen

Shortened form of Gwendolyn, meaning 'fair bow'.

Gwenda

Welsh, meaning 'fair and good'.

Gwendolyn

(alt. Gwendolen, Gwenel)

Welsh, meaning 'fair bow'.

Gwynn

(alt. Gwyn)

Welsh, meaning 'fair blessed'.

Gwyneth

(alt. Gwynneth, Gwynyth)

Welsh, meaning 'happiness'.

Gypsy

English, meaning 'of the Roman tribe'.

Names from ancient Greece

Alexandra
Apollonia
Corinna
Irene
Lysandra
Melaina
Pelagia
Sophia
Xenia
Zenobia

G

Popular Irish names for boys and girls

Aidan	Eileen
Aisling	Kieran
Connor	Liam
Declan	Niamh
Deidre	Siobhan

G

H Girls' names

Hadassah
Hebrew, meaning 'myrtle tree'.

Hadley
English, meaning 'heather meadow'.

Hadria
Latin, meaning 'from Adria'.

Hala
Arabic, meaning 'halo'.

Haley
(alt. Hailee, Hailey, Hailie, Haleigh, Hali, Halie)
English, meaning 'hay meadow'.

Halima
(alt. Halina)
Arabic, meaning 'gentle'.

Hallie
(alt. Halle, Halley, Hallie)
German, meaning 'ruler of the home or estate'.

Hannah
(alt. Haana, Hana, Hanna)
Hebrew, meaning 'grace'.

Harley
(alt. Harlene)
English, meaning 'the long field'.

Harlow
English, meaning 'army hill'.

245

Harmony

Latin, meaning 'harmony'.

Harper

English, meaning 'minstrel'.

Harriet
(alt. Harriett, Harriette)

German, meaning 'ruler of the home or estate'.

Hattie

Shortened form of Harriet, meaning 'ruler of the home or estate'.

Haven

English, meaning 'a place of sanctuary'.

Hayden

Old English, meaning 'hedged valley'.

Hayley
(alt. Haylee, Hayleigh, Haylie)

English, meaning 'hay meadow'.

Hazel
(alt. Hazle)

English, from the tree of the same name.

Heather

English, from the flower of the same name.

Heaven

English, meaning 'everlasting bliss'.

Hedda

German, meaning 'warfare'.

Hedwig

German, meaning 'warfare and strife'.

Heidi
(alt. Heidy)

German, meaning 'nobility'.

Helen
(alt. Halen, Helena, Helene, Hellen)

Greek, meaning 'light'.

Names with positive meanings

Belle – beautiful
Blythe – carefree
Felicity – happy
Lakshmi – good
Lucy – light
Millicent – brave
Mira – wonderful
Rinah – joyful
Sunny – sunshine
Yoko – positive

Helga

German, meaning 'holy and sacred'.

Heloise

French, meaning 'renowned in war'.

Henrietta

(alt. Henriette)

German, meaning 'ruler of the house'.

Hephzibah

Hebrew, meaning 'my delight is in her'.

Hera

Greek, meaning 'queen'.

Hermia

(alt. Hermina, Hermine, Herminia)

Greek, meaning 'messenger'.

Hermione

Greek, meaning 'earthly'.

Hero

Greek, meaning 'brave one of the people'.

Hertha

English, meaning 'earth'.

Hesper

(alt. Hesperia)

Greek, meaning 'evening star'.

Hester
(alt. Hestia)
Greek, meaning 'star'.

Hilary
(alt. Hillary)
Greek, meaning 'cheerful and happy'.

Hilda
(alt. Hildur)
German, meaning 'battle woman'.

Hildegarde
(alt. Hildegard)
German, meaning 'battle stronghold'.

Hildred
German, meaning 'battle counsellor'.

Hilma
German, meaning 'helmet'.

Hollis
English, meaning 'near the holly bushes'.

Holly
(alt. Holli, Hollie)
English, from the tree of the same name.

Honey
English, meaning 'honey'.

Honor
(alt. Honour)
Latin, meaning 'woman of honor'.

Honora
(alt. Honoria)
Latin, meaning 'woman of honor'.

Hope
English, meaning 'hope'.

Hortense
(alt. Hortencia, Hortensia)
Latin, meaning 'of the garden'.

Hulda
German, meaning 'loved one'.

Hyacinth
Greek, from the flower of the same name.

H

I Girls' names

Iantha
Greek, meaning 'purple flower'.

Ida
English, meaning 'prosperous'.

Idell
(alt. *Idella*)
English, meaning 'prosperous'.

Idona
Nordic, meaning 'renewal'.

Ignacia
Latin, meaning 'ardent'.

Ila
French, meaning 'island'.

Ilana
Hebrew, meaning 'tree'.

Ilaria
Italian, meaning 'cheerful'.

Ilene
American, meaning 'light'.

Iliana
(alt. *Ileana*)
Greek, meaning 'Trojan'.

Ilona
Hungarian, meaning 'light'.

Ilsa
German, meaning 'pledged to God'.

I

Ima
German, meaning 'embraces everything'.

Iman
Arabic, meaning 'faith'.

Imelda
German, meaning 'all-consuming fight'.

Imogen
(alt. Imogene)
Latin, meaning 'last-born'.

Ina
Latin, meaning 'to make feminine'.

Inaya
Arabic, meaning 'taking care'.

India
(alt. Indie)
Hindi, from the country of the same name.

Indiana
Latin, meaning 'from India'.

Indigo
Greek, meaning 'deep blue dye'.

Indira
(alt. Inira)
Sanskrit, meaning 'beauty'.

Inez
(alt. Ines)
Spanish, meaning 'pure'.

Inga
(alt. Inge, Ingeborg, Inger)
Scandinavian, meaning 'guarded by Ing'.

Ingrid
Scandinavian, meaning 'beautiful'.

Io
(alt. Eye)
Greek, from the mythological heroine of the same name.

Ioanna
Greek, meaning 'grace'.

Iola
(alt. Iole)
Greek, meaning 'cloud of dawn'.

I

Iolanthe

Greek, meaning 'violet flower'.

Iona

Greek, from the island of the same name.

Ione

Greek, meaning 'violet'.

Iphigenia

Greek, meaning 'sacrifice'.

Ira

(alt. Iva)

Hebrew, meaning 'watchful'.

Irene

(alt. Irelyn, Irena, Irina, Irini)

Greek, meaning 'peace'.

Iris

Greek, meaning 'rainbow'.

Irma

German, meaning 'universal'.

Isabel

(alt. Isabela, Isabell, Isabella, Isabelle, Isobel, Izabella, Izabelle)

Spanish, meaning 'pledged to God'.

Isadora

Latin, meaning 'gift of Isis'.

Ishana

Hindi, meaning 'desire'.

Isis

Egyptian, from the goddess of the same name.

Isla

(alt. Isa, Isela, Isley)

Scottish Gaelic, meaning 'river'.

Isolde

Welsh, meaning 'fair lady'.

Ivana

Slavic, meaning 'Jehovah is gracious'.

Ivette

Variation of Yvette, meaning 'yew wood'.

I

Ivonne

Variation of Yvonne, meaning 'yew wood'.

Ivory

Latin, meaning 'white as elephant tusks'.

Ivy

English, from the plant of the same name.

Ixia

South African, from the flower of the same name.

Boys' names for girls (female spellings)

Ashley
Billie
Casey
Charlie
Elliott
Geri
Jamie
Jordan
Leigh
Toni

I

J

Girls' names

Jacinda
(alt. Jacinta)
Spanish, meaning 'hyacinth'.

Jackie
(alt. Jacque, Jacqui)
Shortened form of Jacqueline, meaning 'he who supplants'.

Jacqueline
(alt. Jacalyn, Jacklyn, Jaclyn, Jacquelin, Jacquelyn, Jacquline, Jaquelin, Jaqueline)
French, meaning 'he who supplants'.

Jade
(alt. Jada, Jaida, Jayda, Jayde)
Spanish, meaning 'green stone'.

Jaden
(alt. Jadyn, Jaiden, Jayden)
Contraction of Jade and Hayden, meaning 'green hedged valley'.

Jael
Hebrew, meaning 'mountain goat'.

Jaime
(alt. Jaima, Jaimie, Jami, Jamie)
Spanish, meaning 'he who supplants'.

Jamila
Arabic, meaning 'lovely'.

J

Jan
(alt. Jann, Janna)

Hebrew, meaning 'the Lord is gracious'.

Jana
(alt. Jaana)

Hebrew, meaning 'the Lord is gracious'.

Janae
(alt. Janay)

American, meaning 'the Lord is gracious'.

Jane
(alt. Jayne)

Feminine form of the Hebrew John, meaning 'the Lord is gracious'.

Janelle
(alt. Janel, Janell, Jenelle)

American, meaning 'the Lord is gracious'.

Janet
(alt. Janette)

Scottish, meaning 'the Lord is gracious'.

Janice
(alt. Janis)

American, meaning 'the Lord is gracious'.

Janie
(alt. Janney, Jannie)

Shortened form of Janet, meaning 'the Lord is gracious'.

Janine
(alt. Janeen)

English, meaning 'the Lord is gracious'.

Janoah
(alt. Janiya, Janiyah)

Hebrew, meaning 'quiet and calm'.

January
Latin, meaning 'the first month'.

Jasmine
(alt. Jasmin, Jazim, Jazmine)

Persian, meaning 'jasmine flower'.

Jay
Latin, meaning 'jaybird'.

J

Jayna

Sanskrit, meaning 'bringer of victory'.

Jean

(alt. Jeane, Jeanne)

Scottish, meaning 'the Lord is gracious'.

Jeana

(alt. Jeanna)

Latin, meaning 'queen'.

Jeanette

(alt. Jeannette, Janette)

French, meaning 'the Lord is gracious'.

Flower names

Daisy
Flora
Heather
Hyacinth
Iris
Lily
Poppy
Primrose
Rose
Violet

Jeanie

(alt. Jeannie)

Shortened form of Jeanette, meaning 'the Lord is gracious'.

Jeanine

(alt. Jeannine)

Latin, meaning 'the Lord is gracious'.

Jemima

Hebrew, meaning 'dove'.

Jemma

Italian, meaning 'precious stone'.

Jena

Arabic, meaning 'little bird'.

Jenna

Hebrew, meaning 'the Lord is gracious'.

Jennifer

(alt. Jenifer)

Welsh, meaning 'white and smooth'.

J

Jenny
(alt. Jennie)

Shortened form of Jennifer, meaning 'white and smooth'.

Jerrie
(alt. Jeri, Jerri, Jerrie, Jerry)

German, meaning 'spear ruler'.

Jerusha

Hebrew, meaning 'married'.

Jeryl

English, meaning 'spear ruler'.

Jessa

Shortened form of Jessica, meaning 'He sees'.

Jessamy
(alt. Jessame, Jessamine, Jessamyn)

Persian, meaning 'jasmine flower'.

Jessica
(alt. Jesica, Jessika)

Hebrew, meaning 'He sees'.

Jessie
(alt. Jesse, Jessi, Jessy)

Shortened form of Jessica, meaning 'He sees'.

Jesusa

Spanish, meaning 'mother of the Lord'.

Jette
(alt. Jetta, Jettie)

Danish, meaning 'black as coal'.

Jewel
(alt. Jewell)

French, meaning 'delight'.

Jezebel
(alt. Jezabel, Jezabelle)

Hebrew, meaning 'pure and virginal'.

Jill

Latin, meaning 'youthful'.

Jillian

Latin, meaning 'youthful'.

Jimena

Spanish, meaning 'heard'.

J

Jo

Shortened form of Joanna, meaning 'the Lord is gracious'.

Joan

Hebrew, meaning 'the Lord is gracious'.

Joanna

(alt. Joana, Joanie, Joann, Joanne, Johanna, Joni)

Hebrew, meaning 'the Lord is gracious'.

Jocasta

Italian, meaning 'lighthearted'.

Jocelyn

(alt. Jauslyn, Jocelyne, Joscelin, Joslyn)

German, meaning 'cheerful'.

Jody

(alt. Jodee, Jodi, Jodie)

Shortened form of Judith, meaning 'Jewish'.

Joelle

(alt. Joela)

Hebrew, meaning 'Jehovah is the Lord'.

Joie

French, meaning 'joy'.

Jolene

Contraction of Joanna and Darlene, meaning 'gracious darling'.

Jolie

(alt. Joely)

French, meaning 'pretty'.

Jordan

(alt. Jordana, Jordin, Jordyn)

Hebrew, meaning 'descend'.

Josephine

(alt. Josefina, Josephina)

Hebrew, meaning 'Jehovah increases'.

Josie

(alt. Joss, Jossie)

Shortened form of Josephine, meaning 'Jehovah increases'.

Jovita

(alt. Jovie)

Latin, meaning 'made glad'.

Joy

Latin, meaning 'joy'.

Joyce

Latin, meaning 'joyous'.

Juanita

(alt. Juana)

Spanish, meaning 'the Lord is gracious'.

Judith

(alt. Judit)

Hebrew, meaning 'Jewish'.

Judy

(alt. Judi, Judie)

Shortened form of Judith, Hebrew meaning 'Jewish'.

Jules

French, meaning 'Jove's child'.

Julia

Latin, meaning 'youthful'.

Julianne

(alt. Juliana, Juliann, Julianne)

Latin, meaning 'youthful'.

Julie

(alt. Juli)

Shortened form of Julia, meaning 'youthful'.

Juliet

(alt. Joliet, Juliette)

Latin, meaning 'youthful'.

June

(alt. Juna)

Latin, after the month of the same name.

Juniper

Dutch, from the shrub of the same name.

Juno

(alt. Juneau)

Latin, meaning 'queen of heaven'.

Justice

English, meaning 'to deliver what is just'.

Justine

(alt. Justina)

Latin, meaning 'fair and righteous'.

Jørgina

Dutch, meaning 'farmer'.

J

K Girls' names

Kadenza
(alt. Kadence)
Latin, meaning 'with rhythm'.

Kaitlin
(alt. Kaitlyn)
Greek, meaning 'pure'.

Kala
(alt. Kaela, Kaiala, Kaila)
Sanskrit, meaning 'black one'.

Kali
(alt. Kailey, Kaleigh, Kaley, Kalie, Kalli, Kally, Kaylee, Kayleigh)
Sanskrit, meaning 'black one'.

Kalila
Arabic, meaning 'beloved'.

Kalina
Slavic, meaning 'flower'.

Kalliope
(alt. Calliope)
Greek, meaning 'beautiful voice'. From the muse of the same name.

Kallista
Greek, meaning 'most beautiful'.

Kama
Sanskrit, meaning 'love'.

Kami
Japanese, meaning 'lord'.

Kamilla
(alt. Kamilah)
Slavic, meaning 'serving girl'.

K

Place names

Ailsa
Alexandria
Brittany
Eden
India
Lydia
Martinique
Normandie
Paris
Skye

Kana

Hawaiian, from the demi-god of the same name.

Kandace
(alt. Kandice)

Latin, meaning 'glowing white'.

Kandy
(alt. Kandi)

Shortened form of Kandace, meaning 'glowing white'.

Kara

Latin, meaning 'dear one'.

Karen
(alt. Karan, Karin, Karina, Karon, Karren)

Greek, meaning 'pure'.

Kari
(alt. Karie, Karri, Karrie)

Shortened form of Karen, meaning 'pure'.

Karimah

Arabic, meaning 'giving'.

Karishma

Sanskrit, meaning 'miracle'.

Karla

German, meaning 'man'.

Karly
(alt. Karlee, Karley, Karli)

German, meaning 'free man'.

Karlyn

German, meaning 'man'.

Karma

Hindi, meaning 'destiny'.

Karol
(alt. Karolina, Karolyn)
Slavic, meaning 'little and womanly'.

Kasey
(alt. Kacey, Kaci, Kacie, Kacy, Kasie, Kassie)
Irish Gaelic, meaning 'alert and watchful'.

Kassandra
Greek, meaning 'she who entangles men'.

Katarina
(alt. Katarine, Katerina, Katharina)
Greek, meaning 'pure'.

Kate
(alt. Kat, Katie, Kathi, Kathie, Kathy, Kati, Katy)
Shortened form of Katherine, meaning 'pure'.

Katelyn
(alt. Katelin, Katelynn, Katlin, Katlyn)
Greek, meaning 'pure'.

Katherine
(alt. Katharine, Kathrine, Kathryn)
Greek, meaning 'pure'.

Kathleen
(alt. Kathlyn)
Greek, meaning 'pure'.

Katrina
(alt. Katina)
Greek, meaning 'pure'.

Kay
(alt. Kaye)
Shortened form of Katherine, meaning 'pure'.

Kayla
(alt. Kaylah)
Greek, meaning 'pure'.

Kayley
(alt. Kayley, Kayli, Kaylin)
American, meaning 'pure'.

Keeley
(alt. Keely)
Irish, meaning 'battle maid'.

Keila
Hebrew, meaning 'citadel'.

Keira

Irish Gaelic, meaning 'dark'.

Keisha

(alt. Keesha)

Arabic, meaning 'woman'.

Kelis

American, meaning 'beautiful'.

Kelly

(alt. Keli, Kelley, Kelli, Kellie)

Irish Gaelic, meaning 'battle maid'.

Kelsey

(alt. Kelcie Kelsea, Kelsi, Kelsie)

English, meaning 'island'.

Kendall

(alt. Kendal)

English, meaning 'the valley of the Kent'.

Kendra

English, meaning 'knowing'.

Kenna

Irish Gaelic, meaning 'handsome'.

Kennedy

(alt. Kenadee, Kennedi)

Irish Gaelic, meaning 'helmet head'.

Kenya

African, from the country of the same name.

Kenzie

Shortened form of Mackenzie, meaning 'son of the wise ruler'.

Kerensa

Cornish, meaning 'love'.

Kerrigan

Irish, meaning 'black haired'.

Kerry

(alt. Keri, Kerri, Kerrie)

Irish, from the county of the same name.

Khadijah

(alt. Khadejah)

Arabic, meaning 'premature baby'.

Kiana

(alt. Kia, Kiana)

American, meaning 'fibre'.

K

Kiara

Italian, meaning 'light'.

Kiki

Spanish, meaning 'home ruler'.

Kim

Shortened form of Kimberly, from the town of the same name.

Kimberly

(alt. Kimberleigh, Kimberley)

Old English, meaning 'royal forest'.

Kingsley

(alt. Kinsley)

English, meaning 'king's meadow'.

Kinsey

English, meaning 'king's victory'.

Kira

Greek, meaning 'lady'.

Kiri

Maori, meaning 'tree bark'.

Long names

Alexandria
Bernadette
Christabelle
Constantine
Evangeline
Gabrielle
Henrietta
Jacqueline
Marguerite
Wilhelmina

Kirsten

(alt. Kirstin)

Scandinavian, meaning 'Christian'.

Kirstie

(alt. Kirsty)

Shortened form of Kirsten, meaning 'Christian'.

Kitty

(alt. Kittie)

Shortened form of Katherine, meaning 'pure'.

Kizzy

Hebrew, meaning the plant 'cassia'.

Klara
Hungarian, meaning 'bright'.

Komal
Hindi, meaning 'soft and tender'.

Konstantina
Latin, meaning 'steadfast'.

Kora
(alt. Kori)
Greek, meaning 'maiden'.

Kris
(alt. Krista, Kristi, Kristie, Kristy)
Shortened form of Kristen, meaning 'Christian'.

Kristen
(alt. Kristan, Kristin, Kristine)
Greek, meaning 'Christian'.

Krystal
(alt. Kristal, Kristel)
Greek, meaning 'ice'.

Kwanza
(alt. Kwanzaa)
African, meaning 'beginning'.

Kyla
(alt. Kya, Kylah, Kyle)
Scottish, meaning 'narrow spit of land'.

Kylie
(alt. Kiley, Kylee)
Irish Gaelic, meaning 'graceful'.

Kyra
Greek, meaning 'lady'.

Kyrie
Greek, meaning 'the Lord'.

Short names

Bea
Bo
Fay
Jan
Jo
Kay
Kim
May
Mia
Val

L Girls' names

Lacey
(alt. Laci, Lacie, Lacy)
French, from the town of the same name.

Ladonna
Italian, meaning 'lady'.

Lady
English, meaning 'bread kneader'.

Laila
(alt. Layla, Leila, Lela, Lelah, Lelia)
Arabic, meaning 'night'.

Lainey
(alt. Laine, Laney)
French, meaning 'bright light'.

Lakeisha
(alt. Lakeshia)
American, meaning 'woman'.

Lakshmi
(alt. Laxmi)
Sanskrit, meaning 'good omen'.

Lana
Greek, meaning 'light'.

Lani
(alt. Lanie)
Hawaiian, meaning 'sky'.

Lara
Latin, meaning 'famous'.

Laraine
French, meaning 'from Lorraine'.

Larissa
(alt. Larisa)
Greek, meaning 'light-hearted'.

Lark
(alt. Larkin)
English, meaning 'playful songbird'.

Larsen
Scandinavian, meaning 'son of Lars'.

Latifa
Arabic, meaning 'gentle and pleasant'.

Latika
(alt. Lotika)
Hindi, meaning 'a plant'.

Latisha
Latin, meaning 'happiness'.

Latona
(alt. Latonia)
Roman, from the mythological heroine of the same name.

Latoya
Spanish, meaning 'victorious one'.

Latrice
(alt. Latricia)
Latin, meaning 'noble'.

Laura
Latin, meaning 'laurel'.

Laurel
Latin, meaning 'laurel tree'.

Lauren
(alt. Lauran, Loren)
Latin, meaning 'laurel'.

Laveda
(alt. Lavada)
Latin, meaning 'cleansed'.

Lavender
Latin, from the plant of the same name.

Laverne
(alt. Lavern, Laverna)
Latin, from the goddess of the same name.

Lavinia
(alt. Lavina)
Latin, meaning 'woman of Rome'.

Lavonne
(alt. Lavon)
French, meaning 'yew wood'.

Leah
(alt. Lea, Leia)
Hebrew, meaning 'weary'.

Leandra
Greek, meaning 'lion man'.

Leanne
(alt. Leann, Leanna, Leeann)
Contraction of Lee and Ann, meaning 'meadow grace'.

Leda
Greek, meaning 'gladness'.

Lee
(alt. Leigh)
English, meaning 'pasture or meadow'.

Leilani
Hawaiian, meaning 'flower from heaven'.

'Bad girl' names

Delilah
Desdemona
Jezebel
Lilith
Pandora
Roxy
Salome
Scarlett
Tallulah
Trixie

Leith
Scottish Gaelic, meaning 'broad river'.

Lena
(alt. Leena, Lina)
Latin, meaning 'light'.

Lenna
(alt. Lennie)
German, meaning 'lion's strength'.

Lenore
(alt. Lenora)
Greek, meaning 'light'.

L

267

Léonie
(alt. Leona, Leone)
Latin, meaning 'lion'.

Leonora
(alt. Leonor, Leonore)
Greek, meaning 'light'.

Leora
Greek, meaning 'light'.

Leslie
(alt. Leslee, Lesley)
Scottish Gaelic, meaning 'the gray castle'.

Leta
Latin, meaning 'glad and joyful'.

Letha
Greek, meaning 'forgetfulness'.

Letitia
(alt. Leticia, Lettice, Lettie)
Latin, meaning 'joy and gladness'.

Lexia
(alt. Lexi)
Greek, meaning 'defender of mankind'.

Lia
Italian, meaning 'bringer of the gospel'.

Liana
French, meaning 'to twine around'.

Libby
(alt. Libbie)
Shortened form of Elizabeth, meaning 'pledged to God'.

Liberty
English, meaning 'freedom'.

Lida
Slavic, meaning 'loved by the people'.

Liese
(alt. Liesel, Liesl)
German, meaning 'pledged to God'.

Lila
(alt. Lilah)
Arabic, meaning 'night'.

Lilac
Latin, from the flower of the same name.

L

Lilia
(alt. Lilias)
Scottish, meaning 'lily'.

Lilith
Arabic, meaning 'ghost'.

Lillian
(alt. Lilian, Liliana, Lilla,
Lillianna)
Latin, meaning 'lily'.

Lily
(alt. Lillie, Lilly)
Latin, from the flower of the
same name.

Linda
(alt. Lynda)
Spanish, meaning 'pretty'.

Linden
(alt. Lindie, Lindy)
European, from the tree of the
same name.

Lindsay
(alt. Lindsey, Linsey)
English, meaning 'island of
linden trees'.

Linette
Welsh, meaning 'idol'.

Linnea
(alt. Linnae, Linny)
Scandinavian, meaning 'lime or
linden tree'.

Liora
(alt. Lior)
Hebrew, meaning 'I have a
light'.

Lisa
(alt. Leesa, Lise, Liza)
Hebrew, meaning 'pledged to
God'.

Lissa
Greek, meaning 'bee'.

Lissandra
(alt. Lisandra)
Greek, meaning 'man's
defender'.

Liv
Nordic, meaning 'defence'.

Livia
Latin, meaning 'olive'.

L

Great female singers

Adele (Adkins)
Aretha (Franklin)
Billie (Holiday)
Dionne (Warwick)
Dolly (Parton)
Ella (Fitzgerald)
Gladys (Knight)
Jennifer (Hudson)
Judy (Garland)
Nina (Simone)

Liz
(alt. Lizzie, Lizzy)
Shortened form of Elizabeth, meaning 'pledged to God'.

Logan
Irish Gaelic, meaning 'small hollow'.

Lois
German, meaning 'renowned in battle'.

Lola
Spanish, meaning 'sorrows'.

Lolita
Spanish, meaning 'sorrows'.

Lona
Latin, meaning 'lion'.

Lora
Latin, meaning 'laurel'.

Lorelei
(alt. Loralai, Loralie)
German, meaning 'dangerous rock'.

Lorenza
Latin, meaning 'from Laurentium'.

Loretta
(alt. Loreto)
Latin, meaning 'laurel'.

Lori
(alt. Laurie, Lorie, Lorri)
Latin, meaning 'laurel'.

Lorna
Scottish, from the place of the same name.

Lorraine
(alt. Loraine)

French, meaning 'from Lorraine'.

Lottie
(alt. Lotta, Lotte)

French, meaning 'little and womanly'.

Lotus

Greek, meaning 'lotus flower'.

Lou
(alt. Louie, Lue)

Shortened form of Louise, meaning 'renowned in battle'.

Louise
(alt. Louisa, Luisa)

German, meaning 'renowned in battle'.

Lourdes

French, from the town of the same name.

Love

English, meaning 'love'.

Lowri

Welsh, meaning 'crowned with laurels'.

Luanne
(alt. Luann, Luanna)

German, meaning 'renowned in battle'.

Lucia
(alt. Luciana)

Italian, meaning 'light'.

Lucille
(alt. Lucile, Lucilla)

French, meaning 'light'.

Lucinda

English, meaning 'light'.

Lucretia
(alt. Lucrece)

Spanish, meaning 'light'.

Lucy
(alt. Lucie)

Latin, meaning 'light'.

Ludmilla

Slavic, meaning 'beloved of the people'.

Luella

English, meaning 'renowned in battle'.

L

271

Lulu
(alt. Lula)

German, meaning 'renowned in battle'.

Luna

Latin, meaning 'moon'.

Lupita

Spanish, short form of Guadelupe. From the town of the same name.

Luz

Spanish, meaning 'light'.

Lydia
(alt. Lidia)

Greek, meaning 'from Lydia'.

Lynn
(alt. Lyn, Lynna, Lynne)

Spanish, meaning 'pretty; English, meaning 'waterfall'.

Lyra

Latin, meaning 'lyre'.

Tennis players

Anna (Kournikova)
Billie Jean (King)
Chris (Evert)
Margaret (Smith Court)
Maria (Sharapova)
Martina (Hingis/ Navrátilová)
Monica (Seles)
Serena (Williams)
Steffi (Graf)
Venus (Williams)

L

M Girls' names

Mab
Irish Gaelic, meaning 'joy'.

Mabel
(alt. Mabelle, Mable)
Latin, meaning 'loveable'.

Macaria
Spanish, meaning 'blessed'.

Mackenzie
(alt. Mackenzy)
Irish Gaelic, meaning 'son of the wise ruler'.

Macy
(alt. Macey, Maci, Macie)
French, meaning 'Matthew's estate'.

Mada
English, meaning 'from Magdala'.

Madden
(alt. Maddyn)
Irish, meaning 'little dog'.

Maddie
(alt. Maddi, Maddie, Madie)
Shortened form of Madeline, meaning 'from Magdala'.

Madeline
(alt. Madaline, Madalyn, Madeleine, Madelyn, Madilyn)
Greek, meaning 'from Magdala'.

Madge
Greek, meaning 'pearl'.

Madhuri
Hindi, meaning 'sweet girl'.

M

Madison
(alt. Maddison, Madisen, Madisyn)
English, meaning 'son of the mighty warrior'.

Madonna
Latin, meaning 'my lady'.

Maeve
Irish Gaelic, meaning 'intoxicating'.

Mafalda
Spanish, meaning 'battle-mighty'.

Magali
Greek, meaning 'pearl'.

Magdalene
(alt. Magdalen, Magdalena)
Greek, meaning 'from Magdala'.

Maggie
Shortened form of Margaret, meaning 'pearl'.

Magnolia
Latin, from the flower of the same name.

Mahala
(alt. Mahalia)
Hebrew, meaning 'tender affection'.

Maia
(alt. Maja)
Greek, meaning 'mother'.

Maida
English, meaning 'maiden'.

Maisie
(alt. Maisey, Maisy, Maizie, Masie, Mazie)
Greek, meaning 'pearl'.

Malka
Hebrew, meaning 'queen'.

Mallory
(alt. Malorie)
French, meaning 'unhappy'.

Malvina
Gaelic, meaning 'smooth brow'.

Mamie
(alt. Mammie)
Shortened form of Margaret, meaning 'pearl'.

Mandy

(alt. Mandie)

Shortened form of Amanda, meaning 'much loved'.

Manisha

Sanskrit, meaning 'desire'.

Mansi

Hopi, meaning 'plucked flower'.

Manuela

Spanish, meaning 'the Lord is among us'.

Mara

Hebrew, meaning 'bitter'.

Marcela

(alt. Marceline, Marcella, Marcelle)

Latin, meaning 'war-like'.

Marcia

Latin, meaning 'war-like'.

Marcy

(alt. Marci, Marcie)

Latin, meaning 'war-like'.

Margaret

(alt. Margarete, Margaretta, Margarette, Margret)

Greek, meaning 'pearl'.

Margery

(alt. Marge, Margie, Margit, Margy)

French, meaning 'pearl'.

Margo

(alt. Margot)

French, meaning 'pearl'.

Marguerite

(alt. Margarita)

French, meaning 'pearl'.

Maria

(alt. Mariah)

Latin, meaning 'bitter'.

Marian

(alt. Mariam, Mariana, Marion)

French, meaning 'bitter grace'.

Marianne

(alt. Mariann, Maryann, Maryanne)

French, meaning 'bitter grace'.

Maribel

American, meaning 'bitterly beautiful'.

Marie

French, meaning 'bitter'.

Mariel

(alt. Mariela, Mariella)

Dutch, meaning 'bitter'.

Marietta

(alt. Marieta)

French, meaning 'bitter'.

Marigold

English, from the flower of the same name.

Marika

Dutch, meaning 'bitter'.

Marilyn

(alt. Marilee, Marilene, Marilynn)

English, meaning 'bitter'.

Marin

American, from the county of the same name.

Marina

(alt. Marine)

Latin, meaning 'from the sea'.

Mariposa

Spanish, meaning 'butterfly'.

Maris

Latin, meaning 'of the sea'.

Marisa

Latin, meaning 'of the sea'.

Marisol

Spanish, meaning 'bitter sun'.

Marissa

American, meaning 'of the sea'.

Marjolaine

French, meaning 'marjoram'.

Marjorie

(alt. Marjory)

French, meaning 'pearl'.

Marla

Shortened form of Marlene, meaning 'bitter'.

Marlene
(alt. Marlen, Marlena)
Hebrew, meaning 'bitter'.

Marley
(alt. Marlee)
American, meaning 'bitter'.

Marlo
(alt. Marlowe)
American, meaning 'bitter'.

Marseille
French, from the city of the same name.

Marsha
English, meaning 'war-like'.

Martha
(alt. Marta)
Aramaic, meaning 'lady'.

Martina
Latin, meaning 'war-like'.

Marvel
French, meaning 'something to marvel at'.

Mary
Hebrew, meaning 'bitter'.

Masada
Hebrew, meaning 'foundation'.

Matilda
(alt. Mathilda, Mathilde)
German, meaning 'battle-mighty'.

Mattea
Hebrew, meaning 'gift of God'.

Maude
(alt. Maud)
German, meaning 'battle-mighty'.

Maura
Irish, meaning 'bitter'.

Maureen
(alt. Maurine)
Irish, meaning 'bitter'.

Mavis
French, meaning 'thrush'.

M

Maxine
(alt. Maxie)
Latin, meaning 'greatest'.

May
(alt. Mae, Maya, Maye, Mayra)
Hebrew, meaning 'gift of God'.
Also the month.

Mckenna
(alt. Mackenna)
Irish Gaelic, meaning 'son of
the handsome one'.

Mckenzie
(alt. Mckenzy, Mikenzi)
Irish Gaelic, meaning 'son of
the wise ruler'.

Medea
(alt. Meda)
Greek, meaning 'ruling'.

Meg
Shortened form of Margaret,
meaning 'pearl'.

Megan
(alt. Meagan, Meghan)
Welsh, meaning 'pearl'.

Mehitabel
Hebrew, meaning 'benefited
by God'.

Mehri
Persian, meaning 'kind'.

Melanie
(alt. Melania, Melany, Melonie)
Greek, meaning 'dark-skinned'.

Melba
Australian, meaning 'from
Melbourne'.

Melia
(alt. Meliah)
German, meaning 'industrious'.

Melina
Greek, meaning 'honey'.

Melinda
Latin, meaning 'honey'.

Melisande
French, meaning 'bee'.

Melissa
(alt. Melisa, Mellissa)
Greek, meaning 'bee'.

Melody
(alt. Melodie)
Greek, meaning 'song'.

Melvina
Celtic, meaning 'chieftain'.

Menora
Hebrew, meaning 'candlestick'.

Mercedes
Spanish, meaning 'mercies'.

Mercy
English, meaning 'mercy'.

Meredith
(alt. Meridith)
Welsh, meaning 'great ruler'.

Merle
French, meaning 'blackbird'.

Merry
English, meaning 'light-hearted'.

Meryl
(alt. Merrill)
Irish Gaelic, meaning 'sea-bright'.

Meta
German, meaning 'pearl'.

Mia
Italian, meaning 'mine'.

Michaela
(alt. Makaela, Makaila, Makayla, Micaela, Mikaela, Mikaila, Mikala, Mikayla)
Hebrew, meaning 'who is like the Lord'.

Michelle
(alt. Machelle, Mechelle, Michaele, Michal, Michele)
French, meaning 'who is like the Lord'.

Mickey
(alt. Mickie)
Shortened form of Michelle, meaning 'who is like the Lord'.

Migdalia
Greek, meaning 'from Magdala'.

Mignon
French, meaning 'cute'.

M

Mika
(alt. Micah)
Hebrew, meaning 'who resembles God'.

Milada
Czech, meaning 'my love'.

Milagros
Spanish, meaning 'miracles'.

Milan
Italian, from the city of the same name.

Mildred
English, meaning 'gentle strength'.

Milena
Czech, meaning 'love and warmth'.

Miley
American, meaning 'smiley'.

Millicent
German, meaning 'high-born power'.

Millie
(alt. Milly)
Shortened form of Millicent, meaning 'high-born power'.

Mimi
Italian, meaning 'bitter'.

Popular song names

Billie Jean (*Billie Jean*, Michael Jackson)
Caroline (*Sweet Caroline*, Neil Diamond)
Delilah (*Delilah*, Tom Jones)
Eileen (*Come on Eileen*, Dexy's Midnight Runners)
Eleanor (*Eleanor Rigby*, The Beatles)
Georgia (*Georgia on My Mind*, Ray Charles)
Mary (*Proud Mary*, Ike and Tina Turner)
Peggy Sue (*Peggy Sue*, Buddy Holly)
Roxanne (*Roxanne*, The Police)
Sally (*Mustang Sally*, Wilson Pickett)

Mina
(alt. Mena)

German, meaning 'love'.

Mindy
(alt. Mindi)

Latin, meaning 'honey'.

Minerva

Roman, from the goddess of the same name.

Ming

Chinese, meaning 'bright'.

Minna

German, meaning 'helmet'.

Minnie

German, meaning 'helmet'.

Mira

Latin, meaning 'admirable'.

Mirabel
(alt. Mirabella, Mirabelle)

Latin, meaning 'wonderful'.

Miranda
(alt. Meranda)

Latin, meaning 'admirable'.

Mirella
(alt. Mireille, Mirela)

Latin, meaning 'admirable'.

Miriam

Hebrew, meaning 'bitter'.

Mirta

Spanish, meaning 'crown of thorns'.

Missy

Shortened form of Melissa, meaning 'bee'.

Misty
(alt. Misti)

English, meaning 'mist'.

Mitzi

German, meaning 'bitter'.

Miu

Japanese, meaning 'beautiful feather'.

Moira
(alt. Maira)

Irish, meaning 'bitter'.

Molly
(alt. Mollie)

American, meaning 'bitter'.

M

Mona

Irish Gaelic, meaning 'aristocratic'.

Monica

(alt. Monika, Monique)

Latin, meaning 'adviser'.

Montserrat

(alt. Monserrate)

Spanish, from the town of the same name.

Morag

Scottish, meaning 'star of the sea'.

Morgan

(alt. Morgann)

Welsh, meaning 'great and bright'.

Moriah

Hebrew, meaning 'the Lord is my teacher'.

Morwenna

Welsh, meaning 'maiden'.

Moselle

(alt. Mozell, Mozella, Mozelle)

Hebrew, meaning 'savior'.

Mulan

Chinese, meaning 'wood orchid'.

Muriel

Irish Gaelic, meaning 'sea-bright'.

Mya

(alt. Myah)

Greek, meaning 'mother'.

Myfanwy

Welsh, meaning 'my little lovely one'.

Myra

Latin, meaning 'scented oil'.

Myrna

(alt. Mirna)

Irish Gaelic, meaning 'tender and beloved'.

Myrtle

Irish, from the shrub of the same name.

M

N Girls' names

Nadia
(alt. Nadya)
Russian, meaning 'hope'.

Nadine
French, meaning 'hope'.

Nahara
Aramaic, meaning 'light'.

Naima
Arabic, meaning 'water nymph'.

Nalani
Hawaiian, meaning 'serenity of the skies'.

Nan
(alt. Nanna, Nannie)
Hebrew, meaning 'grace'.

Nancy
(alt. Nanci, Nancie)
Hebrew, meaning 'grace'.

Nanette
(alt. Nannette)
French, meaning 'grace'.

Naomi
(alt. Naoma, Noemi)
Hebrew, meaning 'pleasant'.

Narcissa
Greek, meaning 'daffodil'.

Nastasia
Greek, meaning 'resurrection'.

Natalie
(alt. Natalia, Natalya, Nathalie)
Latin, meaning 'birth day'.

Natasha
(alt. Natasa)
Russian, meaning 'birth day'.

Neda
English, meaning 'wealthy'.

Nedra
English, meaning 'underground'.

Neema
Swahili, meaning 'born of prosperity'.

Neka
Native American, meaning 'goose'.

Nell
(alt. Nelda, Nell, Nella, Nellie, Nelly)
Shortened form of Eleanor, meaning 'light'.

Nemi
Italian, from the lake of the same name.

Neoma
Greek, meaning 'new moon'.

Nereida
Spanish, meaning 'sea nymph'.

Nerissa
Greek, meaning 'sea nymph'.

Nettie
(alt. Neta)
Shortened form of Henrietta, meaning 'ruler of the house'.

Neva
Spanish, meaning 'snowy'.

Nevaeh
American, meaning 'heaven'.

Niamh
(alt. Neve)
Irish, meaning 'brightness'.

N

Nicki
(alt. Nicky, Nikki)
Shortened form of Nicola, meaning 'victory of the people'.

Nicola
Greek, meaning 'victory of the people'.

Nicole
(alt. Nichol, Nichole, Nicolette, Nicolle, Nikole)
Greek, meaning 'victory of the people'.

Nidia
Spanish, meaning 'graceful'.

Nigella
Irish Gaelic, meaning 'champion'.

Nikita
Greek, meaning 'unconquered'.

Nila
Egyptian, meaning 'Nile'.

Nilda
German, meaning 'battle woman'.

Nina
Spanish, meaning 'girl'.

Nissa
Hebrew, meaning 'sign'.

Nita
Spanish, meaning 'gracious'.

Nixie
German, meaning 'water sprite'.

Noel
(alt. Noelle)
French, meaning 'Christmas'.

Nola
Irish Gaelic, meaning 'white shoulder'.

Nona
Latin, meaning 'ninth'.

Nora
(alt. Norah)
Shortened form of Eleanor, meaning 'light'.

Noreen
(alt. Norine)
Irish, meaning 'light'.

N

Norma

Latin, meaning 'pattern'.

Normandie
(alt. Normandy)

French, from the province of the same name.

Novia

Latin, meaning 'new'.

Nuala

Irish Gaelic, meaning 'white shoulder'.

Nydia

Latin, meaning 'nest'.

Nysa
(alt. Nyssa)

Greek, meaning 'ambition'.

Names of goddesses

Aphrodite (Love: Greek)
Demeter (Harvest: Greek)
Eos (Dawn: Greek)
Isis (Life: Egyptian)
Kali (Death: Indian)
Lakshmi (Wealth: Indian)
Minerva (Wisdom: Roman)
Nephthys (Death: Egyptian)
Saraswati (Arts: Indian)
Vesta (Hearth: Roman)

N

O

Girls' names

Oceana
(alt. Ocean, Océane, Ocie)
Greek, meaning 'ocean'.

Octavia
Latin, meaning 'eighth'.

Oda
(alt. Odie)
Shortened form of Odessa, meaning 'long voyage'.

Odele
(alt. Odell)
English, meaning 'woad hill'.

Odelia
Hebrew, meaning 'I will praise the Lord'.

Odessa
Greek, meaning 'long voyage'.

Odette
(alt. Odetta)
French, meaning 'wealthy'.

Odile
(alt. Odilia)
French, meaning 'prospers in battle'.

Odina
Feminine form of Odin, from the Nordic god of the same name meaning 'creative inspiration'.

Odyssey
Greek, meaning 'long journey'.

287

Oksana
Russian, meaning 'praise to God'.

Ola
(alt. Olie)
Greek, meaning 'man's defender'.

Olena
(alt. Olene)
Russian, meaning 'light'.

Olga
Russian, meaning 'holy'.

Olivia
(alt. Olivev, Oliviana, Olivié)
Latin, meaning 'olive'.

Ollie
Shortened form of Olivia, meaning 'olive'.

Olwen
Welsh, meaning 'white footprint'.

Olympia
(alt. Olimpia)
Greek, meaning 'from Mount Olympus'.

Oma
(alt. Omie)
Arabic, meaning 'leader'.

Omyra
Latin, meaning 'scented oil'.

Ona
(alt. Onnie)
Shortened form of Oneida, meaning 'long-awaited'.

Oneida
Native American, meaning 'long awaited'.

Onyx
Latin, meaning 'veined gem'.

Oona
Irish, meaning 'unity'.

Opal
Sanskrit, meaning 'gem'.

Ophelia
(alt. Ophélie)
Greek, meaning 'help'.

Oprah
Hebrew, meaning 'young deer'.

Ora
Latin, meaning 'prayer'.

Orabela
Latin, meaning 'prayer'.

Oralie
(alt. Oralia)
French, meaning 'golden'.

Orane
French, meaning 'rising'.

Orchid
Greek, from the flower of the same name.

Oriana
(alt. Oriane)
Latin, meaning 'dawning'.

Orla
(alt. Orlaith, Orly)
Irish Gaelic, meaning 'golden lady'.

Orlean
French, meaning 'plum'.

Orsa
(alt. Osia, Ossie)
Latin, meaning 'bear'.

Otthid
Greek, meaning 'prospers in battle'.

Ottilie
(alt. Ottie)
French, meaning 'prospers in battle'.

Ouida
French, meaning 'renowned in battle'.

Ozette
Native American, from the village of the same name.

Color names

Blanche
Coral
Ebony
Fawn
Hazel
Olive
Rose
Scarlett
Sienna
Violet

Popular Scottish names for boys and girls

Aileen	Mac
Alastair	Malcolm
Angus	Rhona
Fergus	Rossalyn
Isla	Saundra

O

P

Girls' names

Padma
Sanskrit, meaning 'lotus'.

Paige
(alt. Page)
French, meaning 'serving boy'.

Paisley
Scottish, from the town of the same name.

Palma
(alt. Palmira)
Latin, meaning 'palm tree'.

Paloma
Spanish, meaning 'dove'.

Pam
Shortened form of Pamela, meaning 'all honey'.

Pamela
(alt. Pamala, Pamella)
Greek, meaning 'all honey'.

Pandora
Greek, meaning 'all gifted'.

Pangiota
Greek, meaning 'all is holy'.

Pansy
French, from the flower of the same name.

Paradisa
(alt. Paradis)
Greek, meaning 'garden orchard'.

Paris
(alt. Parisa)
Greek, from the mythological hero of the same name.

Parker
English, meaning 'park keeper'.

Parthenia
Greek, meaning 'virginal'.

Parthenope
Greek, from the mythological Siren of the same name.

Parvati
Sanskrit, meaning 'daughter of the mountain'.

Pascale
French, meaning 'Easter'.

Pat
(alt. Patsy, Patti, Pattie, Patty)
Shortened form of Patricia, meaning 'noble'.

Patience
French, meaning 'the state of being patient'.

Patricia
(alt. Patrice)
Latin, meaning 'noble'.

Paula
Latin, meaning 'small'.

Pauline
(alt. Paulette, Paulina)
Latin, meaning 'small'.

Paxton
Latin, meaning 'peaceful town'.

Paz
Spanish, meaning 'peace'.

Pazia
Hebrew, meaning 'golden'.

Peace
English, meaning 'peace'.

Pearl
(alt. Pearle, Pearlie, Perla)
Latin, meaning 'pale gemstone'.

Gem and precious stone names

Amber
Crystal
Diamond
Emerald
Garnet
Jade
Opal
Pearl
Ruby

Peggy
(alt. Peggie)

Greek, meaning 'pearl'.

Pelia

Hebrew, meaning 'marvel of God'.

Penelope

Greek, meaning 'bobbin worker'.

Penny
(alt. Penni, Pennie)

Greek, meaning 'bobbin worker'.

Peony

Greek, from the flower of the same name.

Perdita

Latin, meaning 'lost'.

Peri
(alt. Perri)

Hebrew, meaning 'outcome'.

Perry

French, meaning 'pear tree'.

Persephone

Greek, meaning 'bringer of destruction'.

Petra
(alt. Petrina)

Greek, meaning 'rock'.

Petula

Latin, meaning 'to seek'.

Petunia

Greek, from the flower of the same name.

293

Peyton
(alt. Payton)
Old English, meaning 'fighting-man's estate'.

Phaedra
Greek, meaning 'bright'.

Philippa
Greek, meaning 'horse lover'.

Philomena
(alt. Philoma)
Greek, meaning 'loved one'.

Phoebe
Greek, meaning 'shining and brilliant'.

Phoenix
Greek, meaning 'red as blood'.

Phyllida
Greek, meaning 'leafy bough'.

Phyllis
(alt. Phillia, Phylis)
Greek, meaning 'leafy bough'.

Pia
Latin, meaning 'pious'.

Pilar
Spanish, meaning 'pillar'.

Piper
English, meaning 'pipe player'.

Spelling options

C vs K (Catherine or Katherine)
E vs I (Alex or Alix)
G vs J (Geri or Jerry)
N vs NE (Ann or Anne)
O vs OU (Honor or Honour)
S vs Z (Susie or Suzie)
Y vs IE (Carry or Carrie)

P

Pippa

Shortened form of Philippa, meaning 'horse lover'.

Plum

Latin, from the fruit of the same name.

Polly

Hebrew, meaning 'bitter'.

Pomona

Latin, meaning 'apple'.

Poppy

Latin, from the flower of the same name.

Portia
(alt. Porsha)

Latin, meaning 'from the Portia clan'.

Posy

English, meaning 'small flower'.

Precious

Latin, meaning 'of great worth'.

Priela

Hebrew, meaning 'fruit of God'.

Primrose

English, meaning 'first rose'.

Princess

English, meaning 'daughter of the monarch'.

Priscilla
(alt. Priscila)

Latin, meaning 'ancient'.

Priya

Hindi, meaning 'loved one'.

Prudence

Latin, meaning 'caution'.

Prudie

Shortened form of Prudence, meaning 'caution'.

Prunella

Latin, meaning 'small plum'.

Psyche

Greek, meaning 'breath'.

P

Popular names of English and Scottish Queens and Consorts

Anna	Mairi
Anne	Margaret
Catherine	Mary
Eleanor	Matilda
Elizabeth	Victoria

V

Girls' names

Qiturah
Arabic, meaning 'incense'.

Queen
(alt. Queenie)
English, meaning 'queen'.

Quiana
American, meaning 'silky'.

Quincy
(alt. Quincey)
French, meaning 'estate of the fifth son'.

Quinn
Irish Gaelic, meaning 'counsel'.

Foreign alternatives

Eleanor – Elenora, Elinor
Helen – Galina, Helene
Georgina - Jørgina
Margaret – Gretel, Marguerite, Marjorie
Sarah – Sara, Sarine, Zara
Violet – Iolanthe

Q

No-nickname names

April	Jude
Beth	June
Dana	Karen
Joy	May

R Girls' names

Rachel
(alt. Rachael, Rachelle)
Hebrew, meaning 'ewe'.

Radhika
Sanskrit, meaning 'prosperous'.

Rae
(alt. Ray)
Shortened form of Rachel, meaning 'ewe'.

Rahima
Arabic, meaning 'compassionate'.

Raina
(alt. Rain, Raine, Rainey, Rayne)
Latin, meaning 'queen'.

Raissa
(alt. Raisa)
Yiddish, meaning 'rose'.

Raleigh
(alt. Rayleigh)
English, meaning 'meadow of roe deer'.

Rama
(alt. Ramey, Ramya)
Hebrew, meaning 'exalted'.

Ramona
(alt. Romona)
Spanish, meaning 'wise guardian'.

Rana
(alt. Rania, Rayna)
Arabic, meaning 'beautiful thing'.

Randy
(alt. Randi)
Shortened form of Miranda, meaning 'admirable'.

Rani
Sanskrit, meaning 'queen'.

Raphaela
(alt. Rafaela, Raffaella)
Spanish, meaning 'healing God'.

Raquel
(alt. Racquel)
Hebrew, meaning 'ewe'.

Rashida
Turkish, meaning 'righteous'.

Raven
(alt. Ravyn)
English, from the bird of the same name.

Razia
Arabic, meaning 'contented'.

Reagan
(alt. Reagen, Regan)
Irish Gaelic, meaning 'descendant of Riagán'.

Reba
Shortened form of Rebecca, meaning 'joined'.

Rebecca
(alt. Rebekah)
Hebrew, meaning 'joined'.

Reese
(alt. Reece)
Welsh, meaning 'fiery and zealous'.

Regina
Latin, meaning 'queen'.

Reina
(alt. Reyna, Rheyna)
Spanish, meaning 'queen'.

Rena
(alt. Reena)
Hebrew, meaning 'serene'.

Renata
Latin, meaning 'reborn'.

Rene
Greek, meaning 'peace'.

Renée
(alt. Renae)
French, meaning 'reborn'.

Renita
Latin, meaning 'resistant'.

Reshma
(alt. Resha)
Sanskrit, meaning 'silk'.

Reta
(alt. Retha, Retta)
Shortened form of Margaret, meaning 'pearl'.

Rhea
Greek, meaning 'earth'.

Rheta
Greek, meaning 'eloquent speaker'.

Rhiannon
(alt. Reanna, Rhian, Rhianna)
Welsh, meaning 'witch'.

Rhoda
Greek, meaning 'rose'.

Rhona
Nordic, meaning 'rough island'.

Rhonda
(alt. Ronda)
Welsh, meaning 'noisy'.

Ría
(alt. Rie, Riya)
Shortened form of Victoria, meaning 'victor'.

Ricki
(alt. Rieko, Rika, Rikki)
Shortened form of Frederica, meaning 'peaceful ruler'.

Riley
Irish Gaelic, meaning 'courageous'.

Rilla
German, meaning 'small brook'.

Rima
Arabic, meaning 'antelope'.

R

Riona

Irish Gaelic, meaning 'like a queen'.

Ripley

English, meaning 'shouting man's meadow'.

Risa

Latin, meaning 'laughter'.

Rita

Shortened form of Margaret, meaning 'pearl'.

River
(alt. Riviera)

English, from the body of water of the same name.

Robbie
(alt. Robi, Roby)

Shortened form of Roberta, meaning 'bright fame'.

Roberta

English, meaning 'bright fame'.

Robin
(alt. Robbin, Robyn)

English, meaning 'bright flame'.

Rochelle
(alt. Richelle, Rochel)

French, meaning 'little rock'.

Rogue

French, meaning 'beggar'.

Rohina
(alt. Rohini)

Sanskrit, meaning 'sandalwood'.

Roisin

Irish Gaelic, meaning 'little rose'.

Rolanda

German, meaning 'famous land'.

Roma

Italian, meaning 'Rome'.

Romaine
(alt. Romina)

French, meaning 'from Rome'.

Romola
(alt. Romilda, Romily)

Latin, meaning 'Roman woman'.

'Powerful' names

Allura
Aubrey
Inga
Isis
Lenna
Ulrika

Romy

Shortened form of Rosemary, meaning 'dew of the sea'.

Rona

(alt. Ronia, Ronja, Ronna)

Nordic, meaning 'rough island'.

Ronnie

(alt. Roni)

English, meaning 'strong counsel'.

Rosa

Italian, meaning 'rose'.

Rosabel

(alt. Rosabella)

Contraction of Rose and Belle, meaning 'beautiful rose'.

Rosalie

(alt. Rosale, Rosalia, Rosalina)

French, meaning 'rose garden'.

Rosalind

(alt. Rosalinda)

Spanish, meaning 'pretty rose'.

Rosalyn

(alt. Rosaleen, Rosaline, Roselyn)

Contraction of Rose and Lynn, meaning 'pretty rose'.

Rosamond

(alt. Rosamund)

German, meaning 'renowned protector'.

Rose

Latin, from the flower of the same name.

Roseanne

(alt. Rosana, Rosanna, Rosanne, Roseann, Roseanna)

Contraction of Rose and Anne, meaning 'graceful rose'.

Rosemary

(alt. Rosemarie)

Latin, meaning 'dew of the sea'.

Rosie
(alt. Rosia)

Shortened form of Rosemary, meaning 'dew of the sea'.

Rosita

Spanish, meaning 'rose'.

Rowena
(alt. Rowan)

Welsh, meaning 'slender and fair'.

Roxanne
(alt. Roxana, Roxane, Roxanna)

Persian, meaning 'dawn'.

Roxie

Shortened form of Roxanne, meaning 'dawn'.

Rubena
(alt. Rubina)

Hebrew, meaning 'behold, a son'.

Ruby
(alt. Rubi, Rubie)

English, meaning 'red gemstone'.

Ruth
(alt. Ruthe, Ruthie)

Hebrew, meaning 'friend and companion'.

Popular South American names for boys and girls

Atl
Centehua
Citlali
Coatl
Eréndira
Itzli
Matlal
Teiuc
Xochitl
Zolin

R

S Girls' names

Saba
(alt. Sabah)
Greek, meaning 'from Sheba'.

Sabina
(alt. Sabine)
Latin, meaning 'from the Sabine tribe'.

Sabrina
Latin, meaning 'the River Severn'.

Sadie
(alt. Sade, Sadye)
Hebrew, meaning 'princess'.

Saffron
English, from the spice of the same name.

Safiya
Arabic, meaning 'sincere friend'.

Sage
(alt. Saga, Saige)
Latin, meaning 'wise and healthy'.

Sahara
Arabic, meaning 'desert'.

Sakura
Japanese, meaning 'cherry blossom'.

Sally
(alt. Sallie)
Hebrew, meaning 'princess'.

S

Salome
(alt. Salma)
Hebrew, meaning 'peace'.

Sam
(alt. Sammie, Sammy)
Shortened form of Samantha, meaning 'told by God'.

Samantha
Hebrew, meaning 'told by God'.

Samara
(alt. Samaria, Samira)
Hebrew, meaning 'under God's rule'.

Sanaa
Arabic, meaning 'brilliance'.

Sandra
(alt. Saundra)
Shortened form of Alexandra, meaning 'defender of mankind'.

Sandy
(alt. Sandi)
Shortened form of Sandra, meaning 'defender of mankind'.

Sangeeta
Hindi, meaning 'musical'.

Sanna
(alt. Saniya, Sanne, Sanni)
Hebrew, meaning 'lily'.

Santana
(alt. Santina)
Spanish, meaning 'holy'.

Sapphire
(alt. Saphira)
Hebrew, meaning 'blue gemstone'.

Sarah
(alt. Sara, Sarai, Sariah)
Hebrew, meaning 'princess'.

Sasha
(alt. Sacha, Sascha)
Russian, meaning 'man's defender'.

Saskia
(alt. Saskie)
Dutch, meaning 'the Saxon people'.

S

Savannah
(alt. Savanah, Savanna, Savina)
Spanish, meaning 'treeless'.

Scarlett
(alt. Scarlet)
English, meaning 'scarlet'.

Scout
French, meaning 'to listen'.

Sedona
(alt. Sedonia, Sedna)
Spanish, from the city of the same name.

Selah
(alt Sela)
Hebrew, meaning 'cliff'.

Selby
English, meaning 'manor village'.

Selena
(alt. Salena, Salima, Salina, Selene, Selina)
Greek, meaning 'moon goddess'.

Selma
German, meaning 'Godly helmet'.

Seneca
Native American, meaning 'from the Seneca tribe'.

Sephora
Hebrew, meaning 'bird'.

September
Latin, meaning 'seventh month'.

Seraphina
(alt. Serafina, Seraphia, Seraphine)
Hebrew, meaning 'ardent'.

Serena
(alt. Sarina, Sereana)
Latin, meaning 'tranquil'.

Serenity
Latin, meaning 'serene'.

Shania
(alt. Shaina, Shana, Shaniya)
Hebrew, meaning 'beautiful'.

S

Shanice

American, meaning 'from Africa'.

Shaniqua
(alt. Shanika)

African, meaning 'warrior princess'.

Shanna

English, meaning 'old'.

Shannon
(alt. Shannan, Shanon)

Irish Gaelic, meaning 'old and ancient'.

Shantal
(alt. Shantel, Shantell)

French, from the place of the same name.

Shanti

Hindi, meaning 'peaceful'.

Sharlene

German, meaning 'man'.

Sharon
(alt. Sharen, Sharona, Sharron)

Hebrew, meaning 'a plain'.

Spring names

April
Cerelia
Kelda
May
Primavera
Verda
Verna

Shasta

American, from the mountain of the same name.

Shauna
(alt. Shawna)

Irish, meaning 'the Lord is gracious'.

Shayla
(alt. Shaylie, Shayna, Sheyla)

Irish, meaning 'blind'.

Shea

Irish Gaelic, meaning 'from the fairy fort'.

Sheena

Irish, meaning 'the Lord is gracious'.

S

Sheila
(alt. Shelia)
Irish, meaning 'blind'.

Shelby
(alt. Shelba, Shelbie)
English, meaning 'estate on the ledge'.

Shelley
(alt. Shellie, Shelly)
English, meaning 'meadow on the ledge'.

Shenandoah
Native American, meaning 'after an Oneida chief'.

Sheridan
Irish Gaelic, meaning 'wild man'.

Sherry
(alt. Sheri, Sherie, Sherri, Sherrie)
Shortened form of Cheryl, meaning 'man'.

Sheryl
(alt. Sherryl)
German, meaning 'man'.

Shiloh
Hebrew, meaning 'his gift'. From the Biblical place of the same name.

Shirley
(alt. Shirlee)
English, meaning 'bright meadow'.

Shivani
Sanskrit, meaning 'wife of Shiva'.

Shona
Irish Gaelic, meaning 'God is gracious'.

Shoshana
(alt. Shoshanna)
Hebrew, meaning 'lily'.

Shura
Russian, meaning 'man's defender'.

Sian
(alt. Sianna)
Welsh, meaning 'the Lord is gracious'.

S

Sibyl
(alt. Sybil)

Greek, meaning 'seer and oracle'.

Sidney
(alt. Sydney)

English, meaning 'from St Denis'.

Sidonie
(alt. Sidonia, Sidony)

Latin, meaning 'from Sidonia'.

Siena
(alt. Sienna)

Latin, from the town of the same name.

Sierra

Spanish, meaning 'saw'.

Signa
(alt. Signe)

Scandinavian, meaning 'victory'.

Sigrid

Nordic, meaning 'fair victory'.

Silja

Scandinavian, meaning 'blind'.

Simcha

Hebrew, meaning 'joy'.

Simone
(alt. Simona)

Hebrew, meaning 'listening intently'.

Sinead

Irish, meaning 'the Lord is gracious'.

Siobhan

Irish, meaning 'the Lord is gracious'.

Siren
(alt. Sirena)

Greek, meaning 'entangler'.

Siria

Spanish, meaning 'glowing'.

Skye
(alt. Sky)

Scottish, from the island of the same name.

Skyler
(alt. Skyla, Skylar)

Dutch, meaning 'giving shelter'.

S

Sloane
(alt. Sloan)

Irish Gaelic, meaning 'man of arms'.

Socorro

Spanish, meaning 'to aid'.

Sojourner

English, meaning 'temporary stay'.

Solana

Spanish, meaning 'sunlight'.

Solange

French, meaning 'with dignity'.

Soledad

Spanish, meaning 'solitude'.

Soleil

French, meaning 'sun'.

Solveig

Scandinavian, meaning 'woman of the house'.

Sonia
(alt. Sonja, Sonya)

Greek, meaning 'wisdom'.

Sophia
(alt. Sofia, Sofie, Sophie)

Greek, meaning 'wisdom'.

Sophronia

Greek, meaning 'sensible'.

Soraya

Persian, meaning 'princess'.

Sorcha

Irish Gaelic, meaning 'bright and shining'.

Sorrel

English, from the herb of the same name.

Stacey
(alt. Stacie, Stacy)

Greek, meaning 'resurrection'.

Star
(alt. Starla, Starr)

English, meaning 'star'.

Stella

Latin, meaning 'star'.

S

Stephanie
(alt. Stefanie, Stephani, Stephany)
Greek, meaning 'crowned'.

Sue
(alt. Susie, Suzy)
Shortened form of Susan, meaning 'lily'.

Sukey
(alt. Sukey, Sukie)
Shortened form of Susan, meaning 'lily'.

Sula
American, meaning 'peace' or 'little she-bear'.

Summer
English, from the season of the same name.

Sunday
English, meaning 'the first day'.

Sunny
(alt. Sun)
English, meaning 'of a pleasant temperament'.

Suri
Persian, meaning 'red rose'.

Surya
Hindi, from the god of the same name.

Susan
(alt. Susann, Suzan)
Hebrew, meaning 'lily'.

Susannah
(alt. Susanna, Susanne, Suzanna, Suzanne)
Hebrew, meaning 'lily'.

Svetlana
Russian, meaning 'star'.

Swanhild
Saxon, meaning 'battle swan'.

Sylvia
(alt. Silvia, Sylvie)
Latin, meaning 'from the forest'.

Summer names

August
June
Natsumi
Persephone
Soleil
Summer
Suvi

S

T

Girls' names

Tabitha
(alt. Tabatha)
Aramaic, meaning 'gazelle'.

Tahira
Arabic, meaning 'virginal'.

Tai
Chinese, meaning 'big'.

Taima
(alt. Taina)
Native American, meaning
'peal of thunder'.

Talia
(alt. Tali)
Hebrew, meaning 'heaven's
dew'.

Taliesin
Welsh, meaning 'shining brow'.

Talise
(alt. Talyse)
Native American, meaning
'lovely water'.

Talitha
Aramaic, meaning 'young girl'.

Tallulah
(alt. Taliyah)
Native American, meaning
'leaping water'.

Tamara
(alt. Tamera)
Hebrew, meaning 'palm tree'.

Tamatha
(alt. Tametha)

American, meaning 'dear Tammy'.

Tamika
(alt. Tameka)

American, meaning 'people'.

Tammy
(alt. Tami, Tammie)

Shortened form of Tamsin, meaning 'twin'.

Tamsin
Hebrew, meaning 'twin'.

Tanis
Spanish, meaning 'to make famous'.

Tanya
(alt. Tania, Tanya, Tonya)

Shortened form of Tatiana, meaning 'from the Tatius clan'.

Tara
(alt. Tarah, Tera)

Irish Gaelic, meaning 'rocky hill'.

Tasha
(alt. Taisha, Tarsha)

Shortened form of Natasha, meaning 'Christmas'.

Tatiana
(alt. Tayana)

Russian, meaning 'from the Tatius clan'.

Tatum
English, meaning 'light-hearted'.

Tawny
(alt. Tawanaa, Tawnee, Tawnya)

English, meaning 'golden brown'.

Taya
Greek, meaning 'poor one'.

Taylor
(alt. Tayler)

English, meaning 'tailor'.

Tea
Greek, meaning 'goddess'.

T

Teagan
(alt. Teague, Tegan)
Irish Gaelic, meaning 'poet'.

Teal
English, from the bird of the same name.

Tecla
Greek, meaning 'fame of God'.

Temperance
English, meaning 'virtue'.

Tempest
French, meaning 'storm'.

Teresa
(alt. Terese, Theresa, Therese)
Greek, meaning 'harvest'.

Terry
(alt. Teri, Terrie)
Shortened form of Teresa, meaning 'harvest'.

Tessa
(alt. Tess, Tessie)
Shortened form of Teresa, meaning 'harvest'.

Thais
Greek, from the mythological heroine of the same name.

Thalia
Greek, meaning 'blooming'.

Thandi
(alt. Thana)
Arabic, meaning 'thanksgiving'.

Thea
Greek, meaning 'goddess'.

Theda
German, meaning 'people'.

Thelma
Greek, meaning 'will'.

Theodora
Greek, meaning 'gift of God'.

Theodosia
Greek, meaning 'gift of God'.

Thisbe
Greek, from the mythological heroine of the same name.

T

Thomasina
(alt. Thomasin, Thomasine, Thomasyn)
Greek, meaning 'twin'.

Thora
Scandinavian, meaning 'Thor's struggle'.

Tia
(alt. Tiana)
Spanish, meaning 'aunt'.

Tiara
Latin, meaning 'jewelled headband'.

Tierney
Irish Gaelic, meaning 'Lord'.

Tierra
(alt. Tiera)
Spanish, meaning 'land'.

Tiffany
(alt. Tiffani, Tiffanie)
Greek, meaning 'God's appearance'.

Tiggy
Shortened form of Tigris, meaning 'tiger'.

Tigris
Irish Gaelic, meaning 'tiger'.

Tilda
Shortened form of Matilda, meaning 'battle-mighty'.

Tillie
(alt. Tilly)
Shortened form of Matilda, meaning 'battle-mighty'.

Timothea
Greek, meaning 'honoring God'.

Tina
(alt. Teena, Tena)
Shortened form of Christina, meaning 'anointed Christian'.

Tirion
Welsh, meaning 'kind and gentle'.

Tirzah
Hebrew, meaning 'pleasantness'.

Titania
Greek, meaning 'giant'.

T

Toby
(alt. Tobi)
Hebrew, meaning 'God is good'.

Toni
(alt. Tony)
Latin, meaning 'invaluable'.

Tonia
(alt. Tonja, Tonya)
Russian, meaning 'praiseworthy'.

Topaz
Latin, meaning 'golden gemstone'.

Tori
(alt. Tora)
Shortened form of Victoria, meaning 'victory'.

Autumn names

Autumn
Demetria
September
Theresa
Tracey

Tova
(alt. Tovah, Tove)
Hebrew, meaning 'good'.

Tracy
(alt. Tracey, Tracie)
Greek, meaning 'harvest'.

Treva
Welsh, meaning 'homestead'.

Tricia
Shortened form of Patricia, meaning 'aristocratic'.

Trilby
English, meaning 'vocal trills'.

Trina
(alt. Trena)
Greek, meaning 'pure'.

Trinity
Latin, meaning 'triad'.

Trisha
Shortened form of Patricia, meaning 'noble'.

Trista
Latin, meaning 'sad'.

T

Trixie

Shortened form of Beatrix, meaning 'bringer of gladness'.

Trudy
(alt. Tru, Trudie)

Shortened form of Gertrude, meaning 'strength of a spear'.

Tullia

Spanish, meaning 'bound for glory'.

Twyla
(alt. Twila)

American, meaning 'star'.

Tyler

English, meaning 'tiler'.

Tyra

Scandinavian, meaning 'Thor's struggle'.

Tzipporah

Hebrew, meaning 'bird'.

Popular Spanish names for boys and girls

Carmen
Catalina
Diego
Esmeralda
Jesus
José
Juanita
Miguel
Ramona
Santiago

T

U

Girls' names

Ula
(alt. Ulla)
Celtic, meaning 'gem of the sea'.

Ulrika
(alt. Urica)
German, meaning 'power of the wolf'.

Uma
Sanskrit, meaning 'flax'.

Una
Latin, meaning 'one'.

Undine
Latin, meaning 'little wave'.

Winter names

January
Neva
Neve
Perdita
Rainer
Tahoma

Unice
Greek, meaning ' victorious'.

Unique
Latin, meaning 'only one'.

Unity
English, meaning 'oneness'.

U

Uriela

Hebrew, meaning 'God's light'.

Ursula

Latin, meaning 'little female bear'.

Uta

German, meaning 'prospers in battle'.

V

Girls' names

Vada

German, meaning 'famous ruler'.

Vale

Shortened form of Valencia, meaning 'strong and healthy'.

Valencia

(alt. Valancy, Valarece)

Latin, meaning 'strong and healthy'.

Valentina

Latin, meaning 'strong and healthy'.

Valentine

Latin, from the saint of the same name.

Valeria

Latin, meaning 'to be healthy and strong'.

Valerie

(alt. Valarie, Valery, Valorie)

Latin, meaning 'to be healthy and strong'.

Valia

(alt. Vallie)

Shortened form of Valerie, meaning 'to be healthy and strong'.

Vandana

Sanskrit, meaning 'worship'.

Vanessa
(alt. Vanesa)

English, from the *Gulliver's Travels* character of the same name.

Vanity

Latin, meaning 'self-obsessed'.

Vashti

Persian, meaning 'beauty'.

Veda

Sanskrit, meaning 'knowledge and wisdom'.

Vega

Arabic, meaning 'falling vulture'.

Velda

German, meaning 'ruler'.

Vella

American, meaning 'beautiful'.

Velma

English, meaning 'determined protector'.

Venice
(alt. Venetia, Venita)

Latin, meaning 'city of canals'. From the city of the same name.

Venus

Latin, from the Roman goddess of the same name.

Vera
(alt. Verla, Verlie)

Slavic, meaning 'faith'.

Verda
(alt. Verdie)

Latin, meaning 'spring-like'.

Verena

Latin, meaning 'true'.

Verity

Latin, meaning 'truth'.

Verna
(alt. Vernie)

Latin, meaning 'spring green'.

Verona

Latin, shortened form of Veronica, From the city of the same name.

V

Christmas names

Carol
Eve
Gloria
Holly
Ivy
Mary
Natasha
Noël
Robin

Veronica
(alt. Verica, Veronique)
Latin, meaning 'true image'.

Veruca
Latin, meaning 'wart'.

Vesta
Latin, from the Roman goddess of the same name.

Vicenta
Latin, meaning 'prevailing'.

Vicky
(alt. Vicki, Vikki, Vix)
Shortened form of Victoria, meaning 'victory'.

Victoria
Latin, meaning 'victory'.

Vida
Spanish, meaning 'life'.

Vidya
Sanskrit, meaning 'knowledge'.

Vienna
Latin, from the city of the same name.

Vigdis
Scandinavian, meaning 'war goddess'.

Vina
(alt. Vena)
Spanish, meaning 'vineyard'.

Viola
Latin, meaning 'violet'.

Violet
(alt. Violetta)
Latin, meaning 'purple'.

Virgie
Shortened form of Virginia, meaning 'maiden'.

323

Virginia
(alt. Virginie)
Latin, meaning 'maiden'.

Vita
Latin, meaning 'life'.

Vittoria
Variation of Victoria, meaning 'victory'.

Viva
Latin, meaning 'alive'.

Viveca
Scandinavian, meaning 'war fortress'.

Vivian
(alt. Vivien, Vivienne)
Latin, meaning 'lively'.

Vonda
Czech, meaning 'from the tribe of Vandals'.

Food-inspired names

Anise
Candy
Cherry
Coco
Ginger
Honey
Meena
Olive
Saffron

V

Girls' names

Waleska
Polish, meaning 'beautiful'.

Wallis
English, meaning 'from Wales'.

Wanda
(alt. Waneta, Wanita)
Slavic, meaning 'tribe of the vandals'.

Waneta
Variation of Wanda meaning 'tribe of the vandals'.

Wanita
Variation of Wanda meaning 'tribe of the vandals'.

Wava
English, meaning 'way'.

Waverly
(alt. Waverley)
Old English, meaning 'meadow of aspens'.

Wendy
English, meaning 'friend'.

Whisper
English, meaning 'whisper'.

Whitley
Old English, meaning 'white meadow'.

Whitney

Old English, meaning 'white island'.

Wilda

German, meaning 'willow tree'.

Wilhelmina

German, meaning 'determined'.

Willene
(alt. Willia)

German, meaning 'helmet'.

Willow

English, from the tree of the same name.

Wilma

German, meaning 'protection'.

Winifred

Old English, meaning 'holy and blessed'.

Winnie

Shortened form of Winifred, meaning 'holy and blessed'.

Winona
(alt. Wynona)

Indian, meaning 'firstborn daughter'.

Winslow

English, meaning 'friend's hill'.

Winter

English, meaning 'winter'.

Wisteria

English, meaning 'flower'.

Wren

English, meaning 'wren'.

Wynne

Welsh, meaning 'white'.

Bird names

Ava
Oriole
Raven
Teal
Wren

X Girls' names

Xanthe
(alt. Xanthe)
Greek, meaning 'blonde'.

Xanthippe
Greek, meaning 'nagging'.

Xaverie
Greek, meaning 'bright'.

Xaviera
Arabic, meaning 'bright'.

Xena
Greek, meaning 'foreigner'.

Xenia
Greek, meaning 'foreigner'.

Ximena
Greek, meaning 'listening'.

Xiomara
Spanish, meaning 'battle-ready'.

Xochitl
Spanish, meaning 'flower'.

Xoey
Variation of Zoe, meaning 'life'.

Xristina
Variation of Christina, meaning 'follower of Christ'.

Xylia
(alt. Xylina, Xyloma)
Greek, meaning 'from the woods'.

Popular Welsh names for boys and girls

Bronwen	Ioan
Cerys	Myfanwy
Dafydd	Owain
Dylan	Rhys
Gwynn	Siân

X

Y Girls' names

Yadira
Arabic, meaning 'worthy'.

Yael
Hebrew, meaning 'mountain goat'.

Yaffa
(alt. Yahaira, Yajaira)
Hebrew, meaning lovely.

Yamilet
Arabic, meaning 'beautiful'.

Yana
Hebrew, meaning 'the Lord is gracious'.

Yanira
Hawaiian, meaning 'pretty'.

Yareli
Latin, meaning 'golden'.

Yaretzi
(alt. Yaritza)
Hawaiian, meaning 'forever beloved'.

Yasmin
(alt. Yasmeen, Yasmina)
Persian, meaning 'jasmine flower'.

Yelena
Greek, meaning 'bright and chosen'.

Yesenia
Arabic, meaning 'flower'.

Yetta

English, from Henrietta, meaning 'ruler of the house'.

Yeva

Hebrew variant of Eve, meaning 'life'.

Ylva

Old Norse, meaning 'sea wolf'.

Yoki
(alt. Yoko)

Native American, meaning 'rain'.

Yolanda
(alt. Yolonda)

Spanish, meaning 'violet flower'.

Yoselin

English, meaning 'lovely'.

Yoshiko

Japanese, meaning 'good child'.

Ysabel

English, meaning 'God's promise'.

Names from nature

Acacia
Amaryllis
Dahlia
Juniper
Primrose

Ysanne

Contraction of Isabel and Anne, meaning 'pledged to God' and 'grace'.

Yuki

Japanese, meaning 'lucky'.

Yuliana

Latin, meaning 'youthful'.

Yuridia

Russian, meaning 'farmer'.

Yvette
(alt. Yvonne)

French, meaning 'yew'.

Y

Z Girls' names

Zafira
Arabic, meaning 'successful'.

Zahara
(alt. Zahava, Zahra)
Arabic, meaning 'flowering and shining'.

Zaida
(alt. Zaide)
Arabic, meaning 'prosperous'.

Zalika
Swahili, meaning 'well born'.

Zaltana
Arabic, meaning 'high mountain'.

Zamia
Greek, meaning 'pine cone'.

Zaniyah
Arabic, meaning 'lily'.

Zara
(alt. Zaria, Zariah, Zora)
Arabic, meaning 'radiance'.

Zelda
German, meaning 'dark battle'.

Zelia
(alt. Zella)
Scandinavian, meaning 'sunshine'.

Zelma
German, meaning 'helmet'.

Zemirah
Hebrew, meaning 'joyous melody'.

Zena
(alt. Zenia, Zina)
Greek, meaning 'hospitable'.

Zenaida
Greek, meaning 'the life of Zeus'.

Zenobia
Latin, meaning 'the life of Zeus'.

Zetta
Italian, meaning 'Z'.

Zia
Arabic, meaning 'light and splendor'.

Zinaida
Greek, meaning 'belonging to Zeus'.

Zinnia
Latin, meaning 'flower'.

Zipporah
Hebrew, meaning 'bird'.

Zita
(alt. Ziva)
Spanish, meaning 'little girl'.

Zoe
Greek, meaning 'life'.

Zoila
Greek, meaning 'life'.

Zoraida
Spanish, meaning 'captivating woman'.

Zosia
(alt. Zosima)
Greek, meaning 'wisdom'.

Zoya
Greek, meaning 'life'.

Zula
African, meaning 'brilliant'.

Zuleika
Arabic, meaning 'fair and intelligent'.

Zulma
Arabic, meaning 'peace'.

Zuzana
Hebrew, meaning 'lily'.

Zuzu
Czech, meaning 'flower'.

Z